FOR COACH ZACCHEO

FANTASY MAN

ALSO BY NATE JACKSON

Slow Getting Up

FANTASY MAN

NATE JACKSON

A FORMER NFL PLAYER'S DESCENT INTO THE BRUTALITY OF FANTASY FOOTBALL

ILLUSTRATIONS BY TOM JACKSON

HARPER

An Imprint of HarperCollins*Publishers*

FANTASY MAN. Copyright © 2016 by Nate Jackson. All rights reserved.
Printed in the United States of America. No part of this book may be
used or reproduced in any manner whatsoever without written permission
except in the case of brief quotations embodied in critical articles
and reviews. For information, address HarperCollins Publishers, 195
Broadway, New York, NY 10007.

HarperCollins books may be purchased for educational, business, or
sales promotional use. For information, please email the Special Markets
Department at SPsales@harpercollins.com.

FIRST EDITION

DESIGNED BY WILLIAM RUOTO

Library of Congress Cataloging-in-Publication Data has been applied for.

ISBN 978-0-06-247007-2

16 17 18 19 20   RRD   10 9 8 7 6 5 4 3 2 1

CONTENTS

FANTASY MAN

PROLOGUE

THE DRAFT

SAN LUIS OBISPO, CALIFORNIA
"Fuck it. Let's wake him up."

"Dude. It's two o'clock in the morning. We told him tomorrow. He's going to be pissed."

"So what! Nine out of ten is a majority. The time is now!"

"Now isn't a time."

I hear this argument somewhere behind me. My attention is on the ten-by-six-foot fantasy football draft board hanging on the wall. It's made of a giant single sheet of white paper, ordered online, professionally printed. I'm squinting at it with a Bud

Light in my hand. The sheet of paper is why we're all here—
the ten of us—at a rented house a few miles from downtown
SLO. The sheet of paper is why Brian is about to be roused
from a peaceful sleep. It's mid-August and we're on the brink of
our Draft Night, a physical gathering to choose our imaginary
teams for the upcoming NFL season. I've been in this league for
four years now, around the time I stopped playing the real thing.
The first two I missed the playoffs. The last two I won the title.
That's right, folks! I'm the *champion* because I have learned to
play fantasy football with my heart. The experts tell me this is a
bad idea. The experts also have hemorrhoids.

My team is called the Sleeve, and I have the last pick in the
first round and the first in the second—the tenth and eleventh
picks. Previous year's champ picks last.

"I think we gotta wake him up," says Rocky.

Rocky is ready *now*. No one is more upset by my back-to-
back victories than Rocky. He is the commissioner of the league.
He is also the most dedicated football fantasizer, a thirty-seven-
year-old-man who considers knowledge of sports different than
being a good athlete. Rocky is both knowledgeable and athletic,
but considers me only one of the two, as do most of these guys.
They view my back-to-back titles as a black eye on the integrity
of the league, as both years I snuck into the playoffs with the last
seed, then ran the table.

Sure you can *play* the game, Nate, but do you *know* the
game? That means: do you know the *numbers*? No, you don't!

That's right, I don't know the numbers. Me player. Me played.

"Grab me a beer!" I yell and look down at my swollen right
ankle. Pain is my most loyal friend. We were out there in the
dirt field throwing the ball around today. Me, Rocky, and Ryno:
open-field triangle catch. Ryno has a rocket arm. When he cocks
back, I know I can sprint and he can get it to me. *Snap!* It flies
from his fingertips with uncoachable torque and lands in my

hands like a baby being born. I am the midwife. I will not drop your baby!

You would have been impressed by this game of catch. The bunny was! The bunny is brown and has been watching us ever since we arrived here at the turtle house—named for the two tortoises living in the courtyard. Bunny saw the look on my face when the ball was in the air: *total dedication*.

Bunny lives here. I do not.

It's been six years since I've worn an NFL helmet. Time passes like a freight train. Each day I drift farther from the tracks. Farther from the life I lived as NFL Guy, that psychopath who ran headfirst into other people for money. But it never really leaves you; the psychopath. He pops up from time to time, demanding some recognition. But it's getting harder to justify his presence in the real world, where mortality isn't so easily concealed. My body is falling apart.

I'm having ankle surgery in two weeks to clean out a cabbage patch of bone spurs. But you know what? These low-top Chucks felt plenty supportive for a game of catch! Excitement is the best painkiller. And I'm excited to be here at this sprawling rental property on a country road where we all went to college in the late nineties at Cal Poly. We're all pretty excited, honestly. Look at Rocky's T-shirt. There's blood coming through in several spots on the back.

Earlier today, on the last throw, in the last light above us, he nodded to me and took off running like a little boy in the park. I threw it high and deep: predictable, parabolic. Rocky understands this language and gave chase, extending his arms at full stretch and diving. The ball met his hands as he rolled through the rocks and dirt shirtless and popped up like a pro—with a few new cuts. You can tell the athletes by the way they fall. Cheers erupted from deck chairs.

Catch is a spectator sport.

These guys didn't play in the NFL. Didn't play college football. Half of them played high school. Football looks different to them.

This is a yearlong fantasy league with thirteen regular season games. Every week I face a different friend. Then three weeks of playoffs. Top six teams make the playoffs. Top two have a bye in the first round. The championship takes place in week 16 of the NFL's regular season. The buy-in is $100. Winner takes $500, second place takes $200. The high point total each week pays $25.

But this isn't about money. It's about humiliating my friends. And it starts now.

02:04

One hundred eighty draft picks—one hundred eighty names on color-coded stickers purchased ahead of time by Rocky, who also b(r)ought the draft board. Ten teams: eighteen players each. You need quarterbacks, running backs, wide receivers, tight ends, a kicker, a team defense, and one individual defensive player. Basically guys who hold the football. Yahoo, the online platform we use, tracks every intricate statistic— requiring nothing of me but a wi-fi signal.

Each of my player's individual performances score points for my team. Six points for a touchdown, 1 point per 10 yards rushing or receiving, 1 point per reception, 5 points per passing touchdown, and a variety of other single-point rewards for long plays and big yardage totals. The fate of the player's actual football team doesn't matter to me: only the fate of the individual player. One man holds the ball. He's the guy you want on your fantasy football team. He scores you points. But! One man does not move the ball; one *team* does.

Really, the only bit of fantasy advice that I have is this: *Draft with your heart!* Pick the guys you like on the teams you like. Makes it more fun. I won the championship the last two years by drafting with my heart. I pick my friends. Former teammates. Guys I like. I draft wide receiver Brandon Marshall every year. I draft Jay Cutler. Kicker Matt Prater. We all played together in Denver. I draft Broncos. I fill my cup with nostalgia. I try to make it matter!

I played in the NFL from 2003 to 2008 and didn't know much about fantasy football, other than when some friend told me that he drafted me in the last round and said, "Don't let me down, man!"

I definitely let him down.

My career was the opposite of the fantasy. Mine was special teams. Mine was blocking. Mine was injured reserve. Mine was whatever the fuck they asked me to do that week, and it rarely involved the ball in my hands. I had two one-yard touchdowns and 27 catches in my career. That'd be a great single game, but for a career? They aren't Hall of Fame numbers, I'm told.

Rocky leaves to wake Brian and returns one minute later.

"He's up but he's not happy," says Rocky as he laughs and strolls back into the draft room, followed by Brian, golf hat pulled low and puffing from a vapor contraption that looks like a bone from R2D2's rib cage.

"Sorry, man," I say to him. He is unamused. He leans against the wall and looks over his notes. This is his year! He knows it!

Probably not, though. Fantasy football is a crapshoot. It's pin-the-tail-on-the-donkey. Because despite all the conjecture, *injuries* are the deciding factor in fantasy football. The health of the player is all-important. Think of it! We are monitoring another human's *physical health*, so that we may win a computer game. Well then, let us begin!

Twomp-Sack finished in last place one year ago; therefore he has the first pick this year. I played high school football with Twomp. We were both wide receivers in a one-receiver system. T-Sack scratches his whiskered chin with a ponderous look on his face. He is an existentialist with a genius IQ and a restaurant napkin tied around his arm. Fashion, you ask? No. He has a hole in his elbow that split weeks ago on a towel rack and hasn't closed, only widened, exposing marbleized fat cells and scar tissue, white at the bottom. He periodically unties the cloth napkin and checks the pus level, then reties it. We have implored him to seek medical attention. He has implored us to shut the fuck up.

Despite the chin scratching, we know who he wants—the same running back he took with the first pick last year, after also finishing last. Twomp is a Vikings fan. And a Mets fan. And a Charlotte Hornets fan. Twomp's back-to-back last-place finishes are directly proportional to how much of a fuck he gives. Throughout the season, he will make the fewest transactions and tweak his roster the least, often leaving players in his starting lineup who are hurt and unable to play.

Fantasy football requires your attention. If you have something better to do, you will fail. You must monitor the health of your players and scout free agents. You must know who the good backups are. If you don't, you'll be selecting first in our next draft, which you might silently enjoy, because then you can pick with your heart again.

With everyone finally in the room, Twomp peels "Adrian Peterson" off the sticker sheet, puts it on the board, and shoots an imaginary, fadeaway jump shot, kicking out his legs, which are halfway covered by baggy Adidas shorts.

"Brick!" yells someone.

"No, that was definitely in," says Twomp.

Okay, now listen to me, friends. There is a sound coming

from outside. It's a helicopter idling next to the turtle pen. It's an *invisible* helicopter. A *fantasy helicopter*—with make-believe blades cutting through the air. The two turtles are enclosed in a pen of wood and chicken wire. They don't see the chopper. But the bunny sees. The bunny is unimpressed.

NFL commissioner Roger Goodell arrives in that helicopter, along with the first pick of the draft—both of whom are not *actually* here.

Or are they?

Roger walks to the podium with a look on his face.

"With the, uh . . . first pick in, the, uh, 2015 Fantasy Football Draft, Anthony Twomp-Sack Stelmach selects . . . Adrian Peterson, Minnesota Vikings."

And the 2015 fantasy football season has begun!

The door opens and Adrian Peterson (AP) walks in from the greenroom, where he has been with his family. Twomp hugs AP awkwardly and hands him a new Participation Trophy team hat and a jersey with the number 1 on it. Adrian smiles and puts on the hat and holds up the jersey. Flashbulbs and high hopes for the new season. Last year, Peterson was suspended for the manner in which he disciplined his son. Photos of the child's inner thigh were tweeted out and the cyber-mob descended. Are domestic issues private? Is the father-son bond sacred?

Not if you're good at football.

"To new beginnings!"

Number 2 pick: Jack, aka Blue Steel. Jack lives in Santa Rosa, likes red wine and Pearl Jam. Football? Not particularly. His hair is well shaped, his face is clean-shaven, and his shirts are collared. He is getting married next week.

"It says Marshawn Lynch," Jack says, and holds up one of the fantasy football magazines. "What do you guys think? Marshawn?"

"He is a beast."

"Mode."

"Beast mode."

Jack peels the sticker off the master sheet and places the name in the first slot. Marshawn Lynch: Seahawks running back.

"Fuck it, right?"

Number 3: Ryno, aka the Coby Fleeners. Ryno is an All-American kid, blond and muscular and hunched forward like a boxer, but with a refined ear for the underbelly and a keen eye for mischief. And he loves to dance. He pulls on his baby blue hat and c-walks to the draft board with a sticker on his finger. "Jamaal! Don't let me down, buddy!" Jamaal Charles: Chiefs running back.

Number 4: Rocky, aka Ambler Alert (his last name is Ambler). Rocky has full dark hair and stands like he is ready for a fight, but the twinkle in his eyes says different. He is a lover. He especially loves winning. He squints when he laughs but there is nothing to laugh about right now. He didn't even make the *playoffs* last year. Disgusting. He's been disgusted with himself all year. Not again! He sticks Le'Veon Bell's name in his slot, silent as a mouse, and glances around the room at the reaction to his pick. *That's right, motherfuckers!* This is a business trip.

Number 5: Randy Cooper, aka Evil Empire. Randy is the illegitimate third cousin of actor Bradley Cooper. Bradley has disavowed his relationship with Randy. Randy has a bushy beard and long curly blond hair tucked behind the prescription aviation sunglasses that he wears at all hours, outdoors or in. Randy works in TV. No one knows exactly what that means. Sometimes we ask him. His explanations make us more confused. Randy chooses Antonio Brown, Steelers pass-catching machine.

Number 6: Razor, aka Just Win Baby, named after the old WWF wrestler Razor Ramon. Razor is labeled "Mexi" on the draft board. He loves the Raiders and the Dodgers. He is in a room full of Niners and Giants fans. He likes being outnumbered by entitled white people. Good preparation for the *real world*. Razor chooses DeMarco Murray: Eagles running back.

Number 7: Breeze, aka Bruise. Someone called him Bruise instead of Breeze recently and it stuck. He is a vicious emcee. Me and Breeze have been rapping together since freshman year of college. We lived in the same hall. We bonded over Wu-Tang. Breeze got popped smoking weed in his room during the week of welcome (WOW), which preceded the first day of class. He has quietly established himself as a competitive fantasy player. He goes with Matt Forte: Bears running back.

Number 8: Brian, aka Skone. Skone works in finance and has a fiancée and finally it's my fucking turn, he thinks. He's been sober for months and has little patience for drunks. We weren't sure if he'd make the draft, but here he is, Vape-Douche, exhaling a giant cloud of raspberry-vanilla-custard vapor and sticking Eddie Lacy, Packers running back, to the board.

Number 9: Origami Dan, aka Autodraft. Dan is a Bic-bald father of two who drives a truck and used to chew lots of Copenhagen. He used the art of origami to quit his dirty habit and now we find little cranes and Eiffel Towers everywhere after we hang out. Origami Dan chooses Rob Gronkowski, Patriots tight end, whom he sort of resembles.

Numbers 10 and 11: me, aka the Sleeve. Here we go. I was a professional football player. Now I am this. I have the next two picks.

The ceiling fan hums overhead. E-40 rhymes from a boom box: *Marinatin' on the corner with a chip in his phone.* A can opens. A foosball blasts into the metal frame. A belch and a crumpling can. I'm trying to think, goddamnit!

"Your turn, Nate."

"I know, bro." I ponder the lists of names compiled by our little experts, the numbergasm crowd that sells football on television. They rank every NFL player. They make mock drafts. This is their job.

"C'mon, Jackson!"

My heart goes thump. The *heart*! Listen to it! It wants to be heard. Choose with your heart! But the little experts! What about their advice? I must make the right play. This is my season. This is my *life*!

I drop the stack of mock drafts and peel two names off the player sticker sheets and, with the delicacy of a butcher, I place them under "The Sleeve" in spots 1 and 2:

Demaryius Thomas, wide receiver, Denver Broncos
C. J. Anderson, running back, Denver Broncos

"Oh, big sur*prise*! Nate and the *Broncos*!"
"Go fuck yourself, Breeze."
"I would if I could."
Look, Ma, I'm a Denver Bronco again!

02:19

I crack a beer and sit down. It'll be fifteen minutes before it snakes back around to my third and fourth picks. I feel my ankle again. It is irritated from playing catch today. The cortisone injection I got at the beginning of the summer is wearing off.

Okay, I have my third and fourth picks, 30th and 31st overall. I'm looking for another running back and another receiver. That's a solid first-four-pick strategy: two running backs and two receivers. After Origami Dan chooses, it's my turn. I exhale. My friend is still available. My old teammate will be my teammate again! I peel New York Jets wide receiver Brandon Marshall off the master list and put him in slot number 3.

I remember his rookie year in Denver in 2006. He was impressive from day one. Dynamic personality. Genuine smile. Freakish strength. It's been that way all of his life. When one man is given that much power, he struggles to control it; to figure it out, to use it for good, and to let it flourish. B-Marsh has figured out how. He is the Sleeve's most important player. He sets our tempo.

There aren't many guys left in the NFL with whom I played: maybe five or six. I hope to draft three of them. But wait, okay, first I need a running back. Shit! All of the top-tier backs are gone! *Top-tier!* Listen to me, sounding like one of *them*. Hmmmmm. This is where my lack of little-expert name-knowledge hurts me. I want someone durable. Someone big. Someone violent. Someone with dreadlocks!

I choose Joique Bell, running back, Detroit Lions, then grab a beer and walk out into the courtyard to contemplate my next move. Typically I choose my quarterbacks in the later rounds. The four or five best QBs get snatched up early but there are always some big scorers available late. But I don't know, I think I want to shake up the protocol.

I sit down on the patio chair outside. A score of crickets plays in the warm moonlight as the red lighter ignites the green flower in my hand. I inhale and see Bunny standing in the yellow light of a patio lamp next to the turtle pen. He hops toward me, bigger than I thought.

"Hey. Bunny." I exhale.

03:37

"Nate! Your turn!" I hear from inside.

"Coming!" I yell over my shoulder, then look back and

Bunny is gone. I step back inside and I peel the sticker off the list of who's left. It feels good in my hand. I feel something connect.

I stick it to the board.

Peyton Manning, quarterback, Denver Broncos.

"Ooooooo!"

"I don't know about that!"

"Scooby-Douche!"

"You're fucked, man."

I have strayed from my formula. But what is formula but a lack of breast milk? I'm going back to the source.

With my sixth pick, I select catching-machine tight end Jason Witten. We are in a PPR league (1 point per reception). Players who catch a lot score a lot. But Jason Witten's success will largely depend on Dallas quarterback Tony Romo.

Every year this happens in Dallas, and it always comes crashing down on them. The manner in which they deify, protect, and ingratiate the Romo Brand makes him a target. The entire team is always one play from *total* collapse, because of one man. It seems almost inevitable, almost as if they court this disaster—chasing the orgasm of the snapping bone.

So too shall I be then. So too am I always!

With my seventh and eighth picks, I fortify my running back depth by selecting 49er Reggie Bush and Philadelphia Eagle Ryan Mathews. Bush because I'm hopeful that he can shake the injury bug and find success with my childhood team in his native California, and Mathews because we share an ex-girlfriend.

Round nine will be the last of the night. This is a big pick, symbolic of something meaningful, lasting. Aha! I select another Jackson, wide receiver Vincent Jackson, who plays for the Tampa Bay Buccaneers. He is a big receiver like I was. We used to play against each other when he was on the Chargers. He went to college in Colorado. And I saw him once in a club in Vegas.

Basically, he is me. Welcome to the Sleeve, Vinny. Now let's get some sleep!

09:45

Snore, toss, turn, yawn; now I'm sitting on the lawn in the Saturday morning sun. I wipe the sleep out of my eye and realize that I drafted a sure winner last night. Yep! The next nine rounds will just shore me up. The turtles are still asleep, but Bunny is up. He follows us as we walk out to the edge of the field where the Washer boards are set up. Ryno brought them in his truck. Ever heard of Washers? It's like cornhole but with three-and-a-half-inch metal washers to toss and a flat box on which they land. The sound of metal landing on thinly carpeted wood is very satisfying. Washers unleashes the immortal man. When the shiny metal disk is in flight, spinning with precision in a silver arc toward its target, time stops completely, and there is no pain. But it's a four-man game. Only three of us are awake at this moment—me, Randy, and Ryno.

Three-man Washers is a no-go.

"Well . . . hmmm, let's see . . . what do you guys think about . . . Washer *golf*?"

"I like it."

The property is huge. Might as well use all of it! Ryno runs off with one of the boxes. Bunny hops after him for thirty feet, then stops and looks back at Randy and me. I shrug. Ryno sets the board down a hundred yards away on a slight hill, then jogs back like the running back he used to be: tight form, compact, a look of concentration on his face.

We agree on the tee box, which is right where we are standing, then let the washers fly, like diamonds in the sky, catching morning light and flinging it. If only the bunny had thumbs! Silly rabbit, drugs are for humans. By drugs I mean beer. Bunny looks envious but appreciative. We follow the washers with our eyes as they hit the dirt then shoot off in easily detected directions, then we walk the hole in silence.

Randy has a lampshade on his head. Everyone shoots a three. I grab the board and run off to create a new hole, then run back and we tee off again. The disk flies with impressive velocity and I imagine how it would feel to catch one of those washers in the teeth: a row of broken dominoes. Again we all shoot a three. Finally Randy shoots a two and we toss the washers in a pile on the dirt—clink-clink—and head inside. I look back into the distance as the sliding glass door closes. Bunny is standing alone in the middle of the field.

Okay, check this out: Bunny told me two things last night. I'm going to share them with you, dear reader, because it's only right that you know. One: draft Peyton. Can you believe it? *Peyton Manning!* Two: write a book about it. Write a *book* about it, he said. Wow, I thought. I don't know if I'm up for that. I don't know if my friends want to be in a book, ya know? Maybe they just want to live their lives!

Origami Dan is awake now, holding an intricate miniature replica of the Louvre.

"I woke up and this was in my hand," he says.

"Foosball?" he asks.

He puts down the Louvre and picks up two balls. I take one. We look at each other and dump all three into the field of play at the same time. Dan scores two and I score one. Okay, three balls is fun and all—but how about . . . *five* balls? We put one down in the middle of the field and simultaneously drop two through each slot: total chaos.

And a new game is born: Five-Ball.

People file into the game room with coffee to see what's with all the commotion.

"Up for a game of Five-Ball?"

"Five-Ball?"

"Yeah, you haven't heard of Five-Ball?"

"No."

"*Wow!* Really? You don't know about Five-Ball?"

"Should I?"

Rocky walks in holding a wooden sculpture of a dashing rabbit.

"Where did you get that?"

"Don't worry about it."

Is he on to me? Does he *know*? Rocky positions the rabbit on the foosball table's frame to watch over our new game: Bunny Five-Ball.

12:35

Later in that day, we finish the draft, and I load up on love.

10TH PICK: Arizona receiver Michael Floyd.

11TH PICK: Bears tight end Martellus Bennett.

12TH PICK: Bears receiver Alshon Jeffery. Alshon is my "keeper" from last year's team. We get to keep one guy we drafted last year, but must take him two spots higher than the previous year. I took Alshon *two* years ago in the 16th round. Sleeper. Baller. Kept him last year for my 14th pick. Keeping him this year for my 12th.

13TH PICK: Bears QB Jay Cutler. Hey, buddy! Remember me?

14TH PICK: Denver Broncos *linebacker* Brandon Marshall: B-Marsh 2. That's right! We've got two B-Marshes.

15TH PICK: I feel a tug of nostalgia for this pick—this *number*. I was number 15 on the field in high school and in college, and in youth soccer for the South San Jose Lions. When paging my friends from a party in high school, I'd sign the page number 15. I'd like to inject this pick with something extra here today. There aren't a lot of D3 receivers in the NFL. I believe in D3 receivers. D3 receivers have ball skills that their D1 counterparts often lack. D1 is for measurables: your 40-yard time, how much you can bench press, how high is your vertical jump. D3 is for intangibles. D3 is for heart! For my 15th pick, I choose former D3 wide receiver Pierre Garçon of the Washington Foreskins.

16TH PICK: Denver Broncos defense. Everyone needs a team defense. This seems about right for the Sleeve.

17TH PICK: Oakland Raiders dreadlocked running back Trent Richardson.

18TH PICK: Detroit Lions kicker Matt Prater. I played with Matt in Denver. They call him the Hawk. I saw him kick 70-yard field goals at practice.

The Hawk completes the draft. We've got a winner, obviously. The hay is in the barn now. I take a photo of the draft board and text it to my Imaginary Fantasy Secretary, Tracy, so she can get a jump on the paperwork.

Ten men stand around the completed draft board, reviewing our picks. So much promise in all of these names. So much talent. So much hope and expectation. Are they real people? Like, actual humans? We'll never know. But I like to think of them as more than people—sort of like horses! I have hitched my heart to my eighteen horses. I'm holding the reins.

We make our way back outside and pick up the football. Ryno points deep. I turn and run a long angle, pumping my arms, feeling the symmetry of my movements, machinelike. He heaves the ball through the summer sky, and I run to meet it in the wide-open dirt, tractors and junk piles in my periphery, into the symphony of silence.

The ball is in flight and I am the immortal man.

TWO WEEKS LATER

SCOTTSDALE, ARIZONA

Fantasy Football Draft Number Two: I'm in three leagues. Two of them have destination drafts and one is just an online draft—devoid of debauch.

Randy is in this league, too, which is another collection of Cal Poly friends. Randy's beard is still bushy and his aviators are still on as he plays auctioneer to the room. Unlike the "snake" style draft at the Turtle House, this one is an auction, a *live* auction. The results are recorded on laptop spreadsheets by three old Betas sitting at the long communal table in a suite at the W hotel in Scottsdale. Highest valued players go for around $70. Lowest for the $1 at which bids begin. When it's my turn, I nominate a player and Randy runs the show.

There are three Nates in this league. The second Nate plays on my team—kind of like a time share. The third Nate played QB on the Beta Theta Pi football team, which I joined after the real team at Cal Poly cut me. The Alpha Phi sorority's flag football tournament was a highlight of my athletic career. Kegs lined the field. Girls in tube tops and jean shorts clicked their teeth. No beeps or buzzes; no fractioned devotions. Everyone was present. Everyone was horny.

I was looking forward to reliving the old Beta stories with Third Nate but he couldn't make the trip. I'm the only Nate here. I put a thick, square piece of pepperoni deep dish on a paper plate and sit down next to my paper lists of all the NFL players at each position. With last week's draft under my belt, I'm better prepared. But I did no research. I don't know who the promising rookies are. I haven't studied the depth charts. I decide to take a whole new batch of players. Space out my devotions from league to league. Make it as confusing as possible. Players on every team. Give myself more *action*. Don't worry too much. It's all just names on a screen.

12:12

The draft finishes at midnight. We walk out of our hotel and into a Mardi Gras–like party scene off Saddleback, a cluster of fancy bars and clubs. The climate in Arizona allows young ladies no room for wardrobe error. All is on display as we walk through the street: drunks staggering in front of us, high heels clapping along the concrete, golf cart taxicabs idling with heavily pierced girls behind the wheel, steroided twenty-somethings with low blood sugar, cops on horses, and clubs overflowing with enthusiasm for an unachievable moment—an epiphany that will never come. Cart Chick hands me her card and says she'll give us a free ride to an after-hours spot when the bars let out. I take the card, then run ahead to catch my friends, all of them married with children, all of them happy for the few days away.

We walk past the overflowing clubs and into a sports bar at the end of the street, then belly up to the patio railing with drinks and watch the pterodactyls fly by: fake eyelashes, extensions, frilly tops, freshly shaven everythings, thighs rubbing together as she shuffles across the street with shoes in one hand and a cigarette in the other, mascara running and a voice following close behind—"Tiffa-*neeee*!"

Two girls stop on the railing in front of us.

"Hi."

"Why are you talking to us?" says the brunette. "Did we ask you to say hi?"

"You did not."

"Well, why are you talking to us if you're not going to help us?"

"Help you with what?"

"We need to call an Uber."

"Call it."

"We don't have Uber on our phone . . . are you going to call an Uber for us?"

"No."

"Well then get the fuck away from us!"

The next day we go to the W's pool, which is Vegas-pool lite. Bottle service, daybeds, flaming hot sun, tan-as-fuck waitresses in sarongs, misters misting near the bar, pool deck sizzling like a grill, unwalkable with bare feet, bros with heavily trimmed chests, bachelorette parties with matching hats. People drink in the pool. People pee in the pool.

We rent a table area with a U-couch and an umbrella and sit playing bones and drinking beers. Another group of fantasy football dudes have rented out a cabana in the back and are doing their draft right here at the pool in the middle of the scorching hot day. They've hired two girls—Vannah White and Vannah Mexican—to stand up on a little stool and stick names on the slot and giggle. Many hotels are catering to these parties—providing cocktail waitresses, escorts, strippers, whatever—for this purpose.

"Why are you in town?"

"For a fantasy football draft."

This has become an oddly common exchange. Fantasy football is another cultural phenomenon, another sacred ritual, embedded in the game of football. Football is a cash crop, it appears, with no signs of slowing. It fulfills some need, perhaps especially in modern times, as men struggle to find an outlet for their aggression, their inherent need to be masculine.

The American Man is a lost soul. Have a look at him, picking through old memories of power and freedom, lamenting the bed in which he attempts to sleep. It's all on display here at the W pool as Vannah Mexican sips water in six-inch heels and wipes the sweat from her forehead while the men who hired her look around the pool through dark sunglasses to see what people are thinking of this idea. People aren't thinking much except that it's brutally hot and the only solution seems to be alcohol.

We get in the pool and meet groups of naked strangers. I introduce myself while urinating. I feel powerful with this secret. I grew up swimming competitively and peeing in pools. There is no urine-activated colored chlorine pee-detector substance. If there is, it sells poorly.

The day stretches and the sexual tension grows. The girl in the floppy hat and the black one-piece is holding back a panther, looking at me with judging eyes. She is friends with the tattooed yoga enthusiast, who is friends with the two Californian chicks with dark sunglasses drinking whiskey and laughing at our jokes.

"Nate used to be a synchronized swimmer."

"Really?"

"Yeah," I say and pull my leg out of the water and point my toe.

"Wow, that's so cool!"

I've been to this party before.

"We'll be back," say the girls.

"Where are you going?"

"Bathroom."

"Amateurs."

The sun has ducked behind a building. The pool is thinning out. The girls return from the small toilets and get back in the big toilet. A few more toe points and pink lies and we all watch a pudgy dude in regular street shorts enter the pool down the steps and wade over to us with an odd look in his eyes. He has been drinking. We all have. But he is smarting for something. His eyes are bulging. His body language is tense. He starts talking. I stand at a distance, watching.

"How much did these guys pay you to hang out with them?" he asks the girls.

"What?"

"Oh, don't play that shit, I know what's up. Y'all are working girls."

"*Working* girls?" Floppy Hat does not like this accusation.

"Working on a tan," I say.

"Aw, shit, don't believe anything that motherfucker says. He's a fucking liar."

"Me?"

"Yeah, you, fucking fake-ass Brody Jenner."

I draw the line at "fake-ass Brody Jenner."

"All right, man—what the fuck do you want?"

"Wassup?!?!"

I wade toward him in the four-foot water. His eyes widen farther. This is why he came over here. Fine. The moment has turned. Jungle Games. He tenses up, clenches his fists, cocks his head to the side. I lower down to his eye level, lean in, and give him my chin. He hops on two fat feet and takes a wild hook. I dodge it and laugh.

I have ultimate faith in my reflexes. I replace my chin again and give him another chance. I'm not angry, I don't think: just incredibly stimulated. I'm a dog. I want to tussle. He is fat and slow and—*SPLASH*. He comes with a right jab from underneath the surface that explodes like a water balloon in my face. It shoots from his torso and catches me on the left edge of my jaw. He takes two steps back and his eyes nearly bug out of his head.

We have contact, albeit light. But now we have a fight. I hunch down and step forward, ready to end him. Ready to let my best weapons rain down upon his skull and hear his face pop like papier-mâché! Finally a chance to use my fangs! Finally a chance to attack!

But what am I doing? He is a pig in a swamp. I will kill him here.

But he just hit me! I can't let him get away with that. He needs to bleed!

Suddenly, arms pull us both back from the edge and it's all over. Fatty's group is escorted out by security. Good thing it didn't turn into a brawl. They have us outnumbered three to one. The girls on both sides are riled up and argue with each other from across the pool. A few minutes later, as I walk across the pool deck with my adrenaline on one million, a frat boy floating across the pool on a green noodle looks at me and cocks his head to the side.

"Yoooo! You almost got clobbered by cholesterol!"

Yes, I did, bro. I'm fake-ass Brody Jenner.

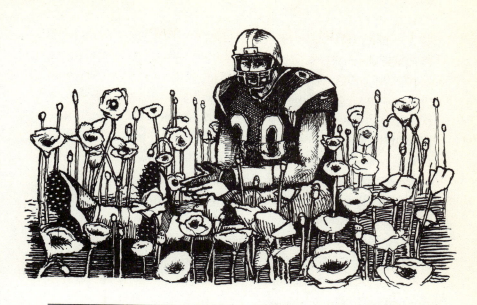

WEEK ONE

POPPY BLANKETS

DENVER, COLORADO

Don't eat or drink anything after midnight, they said, so I didn't. Now I have dry mouth as I walk into the surgery center for my second postcareer operation—probably not my last. I'm an experienced patient. I've had many injuries and several surgeries. Still, I'm nervous. How can one be calm here? Masked strangers are coming at me with knives! I'll be unable to defend myself.

TVs are on in the waiting room while I fill out infinite forms. The morning news says that a TV cameraman and reporter were shot to death on-air a few minutes ago in Virginia. The fourth estate shakes through the screen. Should I call off the surgery? No! Carry on, says a toothpaste commercial.

A door opens and a Voice says my name. I follow the Voice into a room of tiled whites and light blues and change into a gown behind a curtain in a large preop room with several other patients. There are many doctors coming in for the day high-fiving each other and telling jokes. This is another day at the office for them. This is me getting opened like a tin can. I lie on a gurney and the Voice shaves my ankle and I'm happy that it's not my butthole that she is shaving, like it was for my last surgery. Not butthole surgery, but hamstring surgery.

A man with a dramatic, almost theatrical voice talks loudly beyond the curtains about his two daughters—who are both in prestigious graduate schools.

"Well I should *think* so!" he says laughing to someone, while from the other direction, my curtain pulls back, revealing a familiar face. It's Dr. Theodore Schlegel, my old Broncos doctor.

"Hey, Nate! I heard you were in here and I wanted to come and say hi."

I'm happy to see him. Happy he wanted to see me. He was in *Slow Getting Up*. He says he read it after his patients kept telling him he should. He says he remembers my injuries and that there are no hard feelings about how I described the damage; he says that I was fair. We chat about why I'm here, my ankle. Then he talks about a paper he coauthored with several other NFL doctors that asked the league to look into limiting the use of Toradol, the anti-inflammatory injection of choice.

Toradol is a dangerous drug. Players come to rely on it. Ask for it. Makes them feel like Superman. No pain on game day. But it masks the severity of injuries while thinning blood and exacerbating internal bleeding, potentially worsening the symptoms of a brain injury. Dr. Schlegel's no longer with the Broncos, he says. It's for the best, he says.

"Good luck," says Schlegel and leaves me to my gurney. He is quickly replaced by the man with the bellowing voice, the anesthesiologist. No wonder he is singing: he has the bye-bye juice.

"Have you ever had any trouble with anesthesia?" he asks.

"No, I like Ana . . . she was always nice."

"Good," he says as he sticks in the needle and triggers the first wave.

"Have you thought about a nerve block?"

"I'm not nervous."

"That's not what I mean. A nerve block is for pain. It will make your life a whole lot easier postop. I usually recommend it to patients having surgery on their lower body. What we would do is go in through the back of your thigh and inject a numbing agent into a ganglion of nerves that will temporarily—for about twenty-four to forty-eight hours—numb everything below your shin and allow you to get some rest once the anesthesia wears off. Otherwise it can be a pretty tough recovery, especially if they are opening you all the way up." He thumbs through my file. "Which they are."

Sure, I'll take cheese with that. I agree to the recommendation of a licensed medical professional but immediately regret it as he asks me to flip over onto my belly. An IV is hooked to my left hand and tangles under me as I turn. As he ultrasounds the back of my thigh to find the ganglion, he asks me what I do.

"Writer."

"A *writer*? Fantastic! My daughter is attending Oxford this fall on a literature fellowship. Do you have any advice for young writers?"

"Yeah, write for no one but yourself. For no eyes but God's!"

"Hmmm!"

"I have a file in my computer that I write in every day and that no one but me ever reads. And it's the best way to grow as a writer, I think, and to find your own voice."

"That's great!" he says. "That's *really* great. The best writing advice I've heard!" He sticks the needle in. This one does not make me laugh. This is something different. This needle is searching for a vital essence, seeking to snuff out that which makes me *feel*. My leg contracts, relaxes. I shiver; grip the table. It contracts again. I bite my lip and look through the slits in the crinkly hospital blinds down onto Greenwood Village treetops.

"Almost got it! Aaaand . . . there we go." He removes the needle. The Voice next to him says that it won't be long now, that they just upped the dose and that by the time I—

I wake up four hours later in postop. My lips are numb and jaw is sore. Perhaps from Cholesterol's right jab in the Scottsdale Shallows. But also probably from having a tube stuck down my throat during surgery and cocked at an angle that advanced the severity of his chlorinated assault. I drink apple juice and eat crackers. I look down at my foot, naked toes protruding from a well-constructed lower-leg cast. I try to move them. I cannot. I'm paralyzed below the knee. I feel no pain because I feel nothing at all. Goddamned nerve block! I was confused. I want to feel the pain!

America has a dishonest relationship with pain. We want to kill it at all costs. Turn from it. Snuff it out. But pain is instructive. Pain is teacher. Get to know your pain, I think, through slippery teeth as I watch the clock bring me back to life, sliding curtain separating me and some other sleepy shadow. The shadow is a woman. I hear her stirring and sighing. I'm enjoying this slow revival to consciousness. Enjoying the feeling of the drugs wearing off. Enjoying the white tile and light blue voices scuttling about, asking me if I'm okay, if I need anything. I'm happy the surgery is over. I think it went well.

"Is everything okay?" asks the Shadow to the Voice.

"Oh yes, everything is fine."

"What have I been doing? How long have I been here?"

"Not long, we've been checking up on you. You've been talking."

"Oh no! What have I said?"

"*Everything*. You told us all of your secrets."

The Shadow laughs but is terrified by the thought.

That evening, I lie on the couch at home, heavy-headed, foot numb, paralyzed. I'm in no pain—only I'm afraid: afraid I've made a horrible mistake with the nerve block. I stare at my foot, trying to unknot the ganglion and move my big toe. I squint and focus harder. Come on! Just one little fucking wiggle! Show me you're there! But the river is damned. I'm paralyzed for life! A sand blast runs up my leg, through my gut, and into my chest, where it opens like an umbrella and scrapes down my rib cage. My stomach contracts and chills run to my fingertips. I look away. I do not like this. I like pain.

To forget about my paralysis I take the prescribed opioids—NOMNOMNOM—and turn on the TV and watch preseason football. The NFL is a $10 billion a year business. Opioid pain pills are a $15 billion a year business. They dovetail quite nicely as I lie here. The NFL suggests my immortality. Percocet guarantees it.

I try to move my toes again and can't, so I cover them with a blanket and watch *Hard Knocks* on HBO. It's an entertaining show, but I don't know why any team allows them in the building. The reason why no *Hard Knocks* teams can make the playoffs is that God (the ghost of Vince Lombardi) is punishing them for commercializing a sacred process.

But it does give me a chance to see some guys run around. It's one thing to judge a player's worth when all you see is his name on a page ranked by some accountant, but to watch him move gives me a better idea of who he actually is. Football is attitude. Confidence. Some rookies have it, some don't. Often that depends on the organization they play for. Are the rookies empowered or encircled by nonsense? Do they try to teach them lessons or let the lessons teach themselves?

ESPN's *Sportscenter* shows me Arizona Cardinals rookie running back David Johnson running like a beast. He looks strong and fast. Time to make a move. Here is the thing about year-long fantasy football: your team is *never* good enough. There are always moves to be made. You can always improve. This is similar to the actual NFL. Your job is on the line at all times. The threat of being fired is constant. And it's not a veiled threat. It's this: "Nate, if you do that one more time, your ass is going to be on the streets. You got me?"

Yeah, Coach. I got you.

I miss that. I miss being told like it is. I miss having to be my very best every single day. There is no mincing of words in that world. Out here with you guys? Minced and chopped into a fine powder that blows away in the slightest breeze. I suppose that has something to do with the popularity of fantasy football; it's a finite, quantifiable experience with an unchallengeable result in an increasingly vague and noncommittal world.

Through the poppy haze, I pick up the big black phone on my big brown desk and call my secretary for the Sleeve, Tracy. Tracy is . . . well—she's something special. I can't wait for you to meet her. She's been with me for the last few years and was a big part of our back-to-back championships. She wouldn't agree with that, though. She's always so humble, always deflecting the praise to me and to the team. But I'm telling you, Tracy is, just—well, anyway, whatever.

"Tracy?"

"Yes, Mr. Sleeve?"

"Get me Trent Richardson, please."

"Yes, Mr. Sleeve."

"Thanks . . . oh, and uh, Tracy?"

"Yes, Mr. Sleeve?"

"N-nnn-evermind."

Five minutes later, there's a knock and Tracy pokes her head in.

"I've got Mr. Richardson here."

"Send him in."

Trent walks into my office. Powerful guy. Jesus, he was bred to play this game. He has a really nice demeanor. He's worked his ass off for us this last week but I have to make a move here. I have a team to look out for. It's not about me, it's about the guy next to me. You get what I'm saying? I motion for Trent to sit down.

"Trent, look, I know the football season hasn't even started yet, but the season of life has, you know?" I never know what to say to the poor bastards. They've been taught to be so tough, so unaffected. But I know what I'm doing to them. I know exactly where I'm sending them.

"You've been down this road before, Trent. You know its twists and turns. You know the way the tires pop and how the engine burns. You've . . . you've . . . ah, what was it? Help me out here, Trent!"

I'm trying to remember a poem I read once. Give him something he can hold on to. Fuck it. I reach under my desk and press the round black button—about the size of a half dollar—worn smooth from hard decisions like these.

Click!

A pressurized mechanical sound jumps through my mahoganied office and the floor opens beneath him. He falls through and hits the feeding floor with a *bmpfck*, awakening the dogs below. I hear them jump on old Trent as the trap closes with a *whooolsh*, presenting two empty chairs.

That's how we do business around here at the Sleeve. If you can't handle it, this isn't your bar mitzvah.

In Trent's place I sign David Johnson, who skips happily into the office and sits down above the trapdoor.

"Thanks, Coach. I won't let you down."

The Sleeve is complete. Well, almost. The team is right, the name is wrong. People change team names all the time; superstition, hope, attempted humor. Today I'm one of those people. I'm not here to squeeze my players into an old box, chasing the glorious Sleeve of yesteryear. This is a new year. Let us build a new box.

Remember the Bunny? Yeah, me too. How could I forget? We will be . . . Bunny Five-Ball!

SUNDAY

My foot is up and I'm reading the *New York Times*, poppy blankets warm and cozy, morning games on in the background: The song of a football game relaxes me: pads cracking, whistles blowing, fans cheering, coaches yelling; it's lodged in my soul. It'll be there forever. I stop reading and watch the replay of a touchdown. The receiver goes up over the defensive back and catches the ball at its highest point. I miss that feeling. Give me a healthy body and I can do it again, right this very second: perhaps even better.

When I played in the NFL, I was always in such a hurry to run my routes, so eager to please and so scatterbrained. We all were. The game moved so fast because *we* moved so fast: almost in panic mode, trying to impress the coaches. But the older you get, the more of the field you see.

Let's do an experiment. Close your eyes and picture a football play in your mind. Where are the players standing before the ball is snapped? In what formation? What does the cluster of men look like? And where are they standing in relation to each other? This cluster, or formation, is what defines modern offensive football: five fat linemen, heel to heel, one tight end, two receivers, two running backs, and the almighty quarterback. This model has become the only way to play the game. But sitting here with my foot up, wiggling my new toes, I think that there might be a better way.

I take a long pull from my vapor pen and position the blank paper in front of me. One would think that all of the money and attention on professional football would inspire innovation. But the opposite has happened. The model has been restricted, condensed. Coaches are thinking so far inside the box that their penises are turning into belly buttons.

The onus has been heaped onto the overwrought quarterback position. The movement of the ball now almost totally depends on the quarterback's ability to digest an often unlearnable playbook and language, to decipher unreadable coverages, and to do it from the predictable location of a rapidly shrinking pocket that is under pointed attack from trained killers. We are teeing up our quarterbacks and swinging away with a spiked fucking bat. The more we make rules to protect them, the louder they will shatter. There has to be another way!

What we see now on Sundays is the narrowing of the scope, not the widening. Coaches are shuffled from team to team, watch film of one another, stealing each other's plays, operating with identical practice and meeting schedules, administrative hierarchies, and media protocol. It's all the same, only, in the media, they call it parity.

Anyway, I find myself cheering when Luke Kuechly is knocked out of the game in the first quarter with a concussion; that's because my opponent Skone has Luke Kook in his starting lineup. Look at me, making a game of his brain injury from my couch! The same couch I sat on years ago, wearing two pairs of sunglasses because my eyes were too sensitive to the TV light after a brain injury of my own.

During a commercial break, I see an advertisement for Movantik, an apparent cure for opioid-induced constipation. Interesting. This must be a thing. Pain pill addicts can't take a shit; I did not know that. I look at the orange bottle with the white cap sitting on my coffee table in arm's reach. OIC, huh? Lots of pills left in that bottle. Yummy pills. I rattle them and America comes running. I've been taking them for four days and they're taking me down to the bottom of Molasses Lake, friends. I feel the claws sinking in. These are not for me. My bowel movements are too important. I will medicate with herbal vapor instead.

Inhale with optimism, exhale in dread as I watch the Broncos offense struggling. I may have made a miscalculation. The three horses I banked my season on—Peyton, Demaryius, and C.J.— are stuck in the stable. Peyton accounted for a whopping 0.70 points. (Jay scored 17.30 points from my bench, which don't count.) I lost by 15. Peyton may be headed for the glue factory.

Just kidding! No way. It was a glitch in the Matrix. A stumble out of the gate. He'll be fine! Peyton's my guy! He's been through the bullshit before—people prophesying his downfall, firing up the hearse, making floral arrangements. Spite is a hell of a drug.

And anyway, the Broncos got the win. *That's* what matters, right?

Wrong.

Bunny Five-Ball is 0-1.

WEEK TWO

EXHIBITION

LOS ANGELES, CALIFORNIA

"What do you do in there all day?"

"I'm a *writer*! What do you think I do? I masturbate and smoke pot."

Now add fantasy football to the list. Because of the frequency of injuries and the unpredictable nature of game plans and playing time, it is important to modify your approach after week one. Like I already stated, your team is *never* good enough.

The waiver wire is how you pick up the unknown stars who flew under the radar and broke out on week one, revealing themselves as hungry, healthy, bouncy, etc. I had a poor draft in the running back department. My dreadlock theory has backfired. Time to hit the wire.

Each team has a different position on the waiver wire: 1–10. You move up in order when someone ahead of you uses his pick and you do not. So it's wise to save it until you really need a guy. But in order to pick up these hot new players, you have to actually log in and click around for a while. Pay attention. Soak it in. Read up. Look at some statistics. How many yards, how many carries, how many catches, how many tackles. It's numbers. And numbers. Only numbers.

If you are keeping score at home, it's opioid pills: $15 billion; NFL: $10 billion or so; fantasy football: $11 billion.

Eleven billion for fantasy football, you ask? How could that be? Through little bets like ours? No! Daily fantasy sports (DFS). It's the new version of online poker. ESPN, the NFL, and the NFL Players Association (NFLPA) have all invested in FanDuel and DraftKings, the two major DFS companies currently involved in a full-frontal advertising blitzkrieg. Their commercials leapfrog each other during every television time-out, between Movantik (OIC), Viagra (boner), life insurance (death), pickup truck (boner), and beer (boner) commercials.

Newly bearded frat boys tell me that I, too, can win big money on FanDuel, that it will make my life better, that it's "the best adrenaline rush ever."

Adrenaline! That's what this is all about. Something to make me feel like a man.

THURSDAY

The Broncos play the Chiefs tonight in a week 2 divisional matchup. Today I'm headed to the convention center in downtown Los Angeles to participate in a panel at the Cannabis

World Congress & Business Exposition. It's about football and weed—er, I'm sorry—*cannabis*. We call it cannabis now.

It's hot outside. L.A. hot. Sit-in-your-car-and-hate-everyone hot. I take the 90-E to the 405-N to the 10-E and get off at Hoover, then take a left then a right on Venice Boulevard. Venice goes from downtown all the way to the beach: straight shot to the sand if you don't mind driving through the edge of South Central and you've got some time to kill. When I was writing my last book here in L.A., I did have time to kill. Time to murder.

Time used to be a friend. My life was on an itinerary. Everything was scheduled. Punctuality was imperative. "Sense of urgency" was a catchphrase. But when my football career ended, time turned into a bloated corpse that sat in the corner of my room with its plastic eyeballs wide open, staring back at me with a toothless grin. Each tick of the clock echoed into eternity.

So thank God for convention centers! Because of my book I've become something of a marijuana spokesman for football players; I'm one of the few who will talk about it. It's one of the taboo issues that get incinerated in the echo chamber of the solitary writer. The anti-marijuana propaganda simply did not hold true for me, at any time, on any level. It helped me heal. Kept me off painkillers and mentally sharp. It was never more important than my goals. Football always came first.

I've done lots of interviews and panels about marijuana over the last year. Sometimes they introduce me as a marijuana advocate. *Advocate* is an admirable word, I suppose, but it implies politics, which implies going to functions and patting people on the back and laughing at jokes that I don't find funny; saying things I don't mean to people I don't know, wishing to God I was sitting alone in a dark room. The NFL killed my belief in the sacred, folks. I'm sorry. The thing that was most sacred to me—the game of football itself—was placed before me daily and sodomized with a laser.

And they made me watch.

So it is on tiptoes that I have walked into the cannabis game. I want to help my brothers. But I don't want to be someone's shill. Football players have very bad real-world sense. We don't know when we're being used. We don't know how you people live. We don't know how to talk about money. We were bred in captivity. We are being released. We will eat your grandma.

I'm not the only former player involved today. As I ride the upscalator in my black walking boot to the second floor, I see Kyle Turley, former offensive lineman for the Saints and Chiefs. He is hard to miss. He is a towering man and walks with a cane after a life spent playing football, and lately has been vocal about the therapeutic benefits of cannabis. He has a filmmaker following him today named Sean Pamphilon. Sean broke the "Bountygate" story a few years back, releasing an audiotape of a Saints tough-guy coach using head-targeting rhetoric in a pre-game locker room speech. The league suspended several players for multiple games and coach Sean Payton for the entire season. It's okay to hurt someone on the football field—it's okay to kill him, actually—unless you *try* to, that is.

Here, Timmy, hit him as hard as you can with this bat. Go ahead! Don't be a little pussy, Timmy. Hit him! But don't try to *hurt* him. Understand? But hit him . . . hard. *Harder!* But if you *intentionally* hurt him, well, I'm sorry but that type of behavior is detrimental to the integrity of the league and will not be tolerated. Now hit him again . . . *harder!*

Kyle and I walk to the front of the auditorium, ascend a small set of stairs, and sit down at a long, folding table. We are sharing the stage with several marijuana industry professionals: neurologists, doctors, growers. There is a microphone in front of each of us.

Next to me onstage is Joel Stanley, CEO of CW Botanicals. His company makes a product called Charlotte's Web. It is a hemp oil that is extracted from a specific strain of plant—high in cannabidiols (CBDs) and low in THC. These are terms I'm learning about. It's a new language for me. THC is what produces the high that is generally associated with cannabis use. The high is what scares people. Getting high is not what Charlotte's Web is about. Getting healthy is. The therapeutic benefits of CBDs seem to be manifold, but are still largely unknown due to cannabis's status as a Schedule 1 drug in this country. Schedule 1 drugs are considered to have no medicinal value and therefore are not easily studied. Coupled with the stigma that comes with smoking it, the acceptance of cannabis as a medicine has moved along at a crawl.

But during panels like this, I see why the pace is quickening. All I have are my own experiences, but my silent epiphanies are given a lift in the presence of medical professionals who trumpet cannabis as an effective pain medication, sleep aid, anti-inflammatory, appetite stimulant, and anticonvulsant. I kicked the pain pills after only a few days and have been medicating with cannabis for the last few weeks. My ankle is no longer swollen and is healing ahead of schedule.

My fellow panelists talk about their pill addiction and something in your body called the endocannabinoid system, which I'm hearing about for the first time.

As the question-and-answer portion begins, a portly middle-aged man finally gets the microphone. He's been fidgeting and shifting in his seat the whole time. He wants to say something. Not without effort, he stands and addresses the panel.

"Listen, I'm a doctor. I own fifty dispensaries now," he says, "but I used to work with doctors and trainers for the NFL, and I'm telling you, they're *never* gonna listen to what you guys are saying here. You don't stand a chance. They don't *care* about you guys. Don't you get it? You're just a number to them. There's no way that you—"

"You see what I mean, folks?" I interrupt him. "This is what we're up against!"

"Oh no! I'm on *your* side! I'm just playing devil's advocate here."

"Oh yeah? You know, it's that mentality that—"

We start talking over each other and I get very worked up. This sweet man has just awakened something in me. I see in him everything that is wrong with the NFL, everything that made me an obedient soldier, everything that told me to "shut up and play," every voice that put profit over humanity, every old man who points to a brick wall and tells me to run into it, again. I feel my skin flush. The room smalls. Doctor ducks behind someone's head. What must I look like? Geez. This is not how I want to be perceived. I'm a pacifist now! The moment passes. Someone else speaks, the conversation corrects itself amicably, and the room resumes its order. My heartbeat slows. Douchey Howser, M.D. won't look at me.

When the panel concludes to applause, I descend the stairs and stand in front of the stage, collecting business cards from the surprisingly large number of marijuana entrepreneurs in attendance. I smile and nod but these are going in the trash. I want to write books and play guitar, not talk about weed all day.

The good doctor approaches me sheepishly. I smile at him and we hug it out. He is not a bad guy. I put my arm around his shoulder as we walk toward the back. I don't want to hurt him. I just . . . we are interrupted by a tan and glowing cannabis lady. She was listening to us attentively. She had something on her mind. Something best discussed in private. She gives me her card. This one will not go in the trash.

SUNDAY

Went to bed early last night and slept like a stone. Slept like the moon. Slept like sperm in balls. Waking up refreshed on the weekend is its own sort of pleasure. My friend asked me if I wanted to go out last night. "There's some party, supposedly," he said.

I always enjoyed a good party. It leveled the scales, gave me control of my power. But too much alcohol makes you slow. And going into work hungover in the NFL is a bad idea. You make yourself vulnerable. Too many eyes on you. Too much pressure. But marijuana is different. The first time I tried it was one month before I ever put on a football helmet. It was the summer before my freshman year. The plant took to me rightly. Once I discovered it, I became more focused, more empathetic, less disruptive, and more creative. Same goes for a lot of professional football players. They made it to the NFL, after all. They are the best head-smashers in the world! Let's study their brains!

Anyway, the morning games start in thirty minutes. I'm going to sit down and watch them. But first, a bit of fantasy football gamesmanship for you to ponder: my opponent, Randy Cooper, who is traveling in Europe with his wife, has tight end Delanie Walker in his starting lineup. I see on my computer here that Delanie Walker is inactive. Randy is obviously busy; otherwise he would replace Delanie with an active player. Delanie will score him zero points today, which will greatly improve Bunny Five-Ball's chance at victory. But there is such a thing as ethics in competition, right? And besides, I want your best shot! I don't want to beat you when you're shorthanded, or not paying attention.

So, do I tell him or not?

I do not. I'm not a babysitter.

Maybe I should be. The day does not bring me good tidings. The fantasy gods are angry. Bunny Five-Ball, reigning champion, is off to a rough start: 0-2.

WEEK THREE

NAME CHANGE

VENICE, CALIFORNIA

I woke up early this morning and immediately checked to see if I got Washington Foreskins rookie running back Matt Jones on the waiver wire. He had three touchdowns on Sunday. He was rated high, very high. And I was eighth on the wire, so I didn't get him.

Instead, I'm stuck with a still-depleted running back squad. Bunny Five-Ball needs some new mojo. I love Matt Prater. He is my friend. But the Detroit Lions are not moving the ball. He can't kick it through the goal posts if they don't cross the fifty-yard line. So I have to ax the Hawk. Jay Cutler, too, actually. Jay hurt himself in the game. I've been starting Peyton. Did I mention I am 0-2?

I'm 0-2.

You don't *really* need a second quarterback on your fantasy team; just like you don't *really* need a third quarterback on your actual team. But I keep Jay around because, unlike most of these bastards, I understand a little thing called *loyalty*. He captained my ship on and off for the last two seasons—both of them championships. I take care of my guys. I don't forget their sacrifices. But even Jay would admit that he's no use to me hurt. And actually, it's probably better for both of us that he's not on the team, at least not while Peyton is upright and I have a running back void to fill. The more running backs I can put on my roster, the more likely one of them will pop.

"Tracy?"

"Yes, Mr. Sleeve?"

"Call me Mr. Five-Ball from now on, okay?"

"Yes, Mr. Five-Ball."

"Send in Jay and Matt, wouldja?"

"Yes, Mr. Five-Ball."

"Oh, and, uh, Tracy?"

"Yes, Mr. Five-Ball?"

"Tell them to bring their playbooks."

Jay walks in, holding a giant sea scroll. Matt walks in empty-handed, as kickers don't have plays, other than *kicks*. I stand to greet them, pulling my mesh shorts from my ass crack. My movement stirs up my BO, which follows me around the desk as I shake their hands and motion for them to sit. They sit down in adjacent chairs and I sit across from them and adjust my visor. I pick up a can and spit in it. I usually like cutting my players one at a time, but both chairs are wired to the same mechanism, and considering we all know each other, I thought we could have a moment before getting down to business. Thing is, they walk in with blank stares. No memory of me whatsoever. Ha!

"Tracy! Tracy! Hold my calls, okay? What?"

"I didn't say anything, Mr. Five-Ball."

"Exactly!" I hang up the phone. "Tracy is the best, huh? You see the, uh, huh huh, sweater she's wearing?"

"She's not wearing a sweater, Coach."

"Exactly!" My attempt at humor falls flat. I need to make this quick.

"Well, fellas . . . I'll just get right to it. This is the end of the line for us . . . for you . . . and for me. This is where we part hairs. This is where we separate the men from the guys. This is where we say 'mahalo.' This is where . . . look, I don't like this any more than you do. Hell, I know you gave me your all out there. I know you guys can play in this league. But, well, we've decided to go in another direction. You understand this business. Nothing personal."

Click!

"You motherfu—" Jay's voice drops out.

"What was that, Jay? I couldn't hear you."

Now—who am I going to pick up in their place?

"Tracy, get me Tom Brady on the line. What? Yeah, I know, Tracy. I've got something I want to ask him."

I have my eye on his teammate, Dion Lewis. Dion is a young running back for the New England Patriots—Colonial America's Team—and he's available if I want him. But I'm not just going to sign him off the streets. Every good GM does his homework. If I lived in his city, I'd find his house and go steal his trash, pour it out in my kitchen, and figure out what this kid is really up to. I did that last year during the playoffs with two of my starters. It worked. I found out what I needed to know, and a bit more. I also had to replace my kitchen table. My wife moved out after that one. She took the kids. They'll be back.

"Mr. Five-Ball, I have Tom Brady on the line."

"Tracy, have I ever told you that I couldn't do this without you?"

"Yes, Mr. Five-Ball."

"Give yourself the afternoon off."

"It's six p.m."

"Oh, and, uh, Tracy!"

"Yes, Mr. Five-Ball?"

"Wear something yellow tomorrow, could you?"

I click over.

"Tommy Boy! Shit's on fire, am I right?"

"Excuse me?"

Tommy gets me. We talk for a while. Our conversation puts me at ease. Tommy says Dion looks great. Says he's ready to go. Says he's learned the Patriot Way. Does his job, Tommy says. Knows his role. Plays hard. Knows all of his plays and hasn't been late once. Had a good game last Sunday and handled the media well all week. Very coachable, Tommy says. Belichick loves him, Tommy says. Sleeps in a hyperbaric chamber. Virgin, never been with a woman. Never had a drop of alcohol. Never watched porn, either, Tommy says. Never been to a bar. Doesn't watch TV; watches game film. Doesn't go to parties. Stays home and reads the playbook. Doesn't own a cell phone. Speaks in beeps and clicks, Tommy says. Has never smiled. Not once. Derives no joy whatsoever from any of this at all. True professional.

This is what I need. I hang up, log on, and cut bait. In place of Jay Cutler, I bring on Dion Lewis. And in place of Matt Prater, I bring on new Broncos kicker Brandon McManus, who has likely never been called McmAnus. (I can't wait until McDonald's brings it back this Christmas!) He's been crushing the ball.

But here I am picking with my heart again: putting more

eggs in the orange basket. Denver kickers are always a good bet, though. They get a lot of chances and the ball carries in the thin air. Have you even been to Denver? Have you had sex there? If you have, you came immediately. But now you're in the mile-high club! Insinuate it in a rambling Facebook post and watch your problems evaporate.

There is one more thing that is troubling me, though: *Bunny Five-Ball*. The name. It's just, I don't know, something isn't right with it. It feels like I'm forcing it, trying to be too cute. Well, the fantasy gods do not appreciate cute. The Sleeve brought me good tidings the last two years, and here I ditch the moniker in favor of a fly-by-night rabbit that couldn't pick me out of a lineup? I don't know. I'm just being sensitive. I still believe in that bunny. The bunny stays.

We are *Bunny Sleeve*.

THURSDAY

I used to think that on Thursday night games, since everyone's legs were so tired from the previous Sunday, the passing game would be weak and teams would rely on their running backs to carry the load. But I'm realizing that the opposite might be true. Games are hard on running backs. It takes them the entire week to recover. Monday and Tuesday are do-nothing days in the NFL. Recover from the car crash days. Let the brain swelling go down days. Stress-free days. Smoke weed days. But when you play Thursday, you don't get those vital recovery days off.

Thursday night games are CTE factories.

Bodies slamming into bodies over and over again, brutalizing flesh and bone, obscured under shiny pads, superhero spandex garments and clever television production. But underneath the logos, the body bleeds. Players have no choice but to play on the day the game is scheduled, and then to run the plays that are called. They are contractually obligated to attack on certain dates, but the body is crying out for rest.

But *rest* is a dirty word in the NFL. And the eye of judgment never blinks. There are too many stakes in the ground to allow these guys to take their foot off the gas. But this road has twists and turns. We are taking the corners too fast.

"Yay!" says ESPN. "More crashes, please!"

There are twenty-two football players on the field at once. As the game grows, attracting more eyeballs, more sponsors, more advertisers, more merchandisers, more fans, more cameras, more journalists, the twenty-two players on the field bear a bigger burden. Every new eyeball has something at stake—often a monetary investment. And the league wants to make its customers happy.

Fine, then, steer me back into the car crash, but tonight it is with less gas in the tank—like it or not. That's why I now think that a simple passing game is what wins you Thursday night games. Give it to your best receivers on basic routes and let them move the chains. Remember Matt Jones? He was the hot commodity on the waiver wire after his three-touchdown performance on Sunday. Four days later he put on his pads and got wigwomped against the Giants. His body was already hamburger meat. The fantasy winners of the night were Eli Manning and his two wide receivers, Odell Beckham Jr. and Ruben Randall, who cut up the Foreskins zone defense with relative ease.

Three games in the books for these two teams, both 1-2 now. The Giants were 0-2 going into the game and were subjected to the "must win" media chatter this week. Statistics about the unlikelihood of 0-2 teams making the playoffs were trotted out. Earnest roundtable discussions ensued.

Whose season is over? Who is dead? So eager to bury bodies, aren't we? Funerals get good ratings, I guess.

SUNDAY

I'm in the Venice sun holding a chocolate croissant and no one is trying to take it from me. I wish someone would try! Sunday mornings are different for me now: sleepier, less urgent. Riding my bike for coffee and donuts. Stopping to talk with neighbors. Petting dogs. Looking at tables of fruit. Listening to music in my headphones. Getting a newspaper. A little sunshine. A little movement. A little . . . Parinda, the new owner of a coffee shop I like, called Self Espresso.

She's trying to clean it up, kick out the vagrants and transients who used to frequent the place. I understand why but I wish she'd let them stay. They're mostly gone now, but it's still a good place to write. Two floors, high ceilings, sturdy tables and chairs, shelves full of books, local art on the wall, and it still smells of the unattached; gnats hovering, fans blowing, and always a little muggy, especially upstairs.

"It's organic," Parinda says about her coffee. "Best-kept secret . . . but I don't want it to be a secret. I want people to come!" This will be a struggle at first. It's something that is happening in Venice, like in other *cool* parts of California. Money is moving in and pushing out the old flavor that made the place savory in the first place. You know the story.

The freaks are no longer wanted. The last owner was a wealthy duo who didn't care much about gentrification. They let a group of gritty kids run it. They hired troubled young baristas with tattoos and stars in their eyes. They'd call you "man" and laugh a lot. They sympathized with the Venice street folks who often used the bathroom to freshen up, or fell asleep upstairs, or spread a collection of garbage on one of the tables, then disappeared. Or who sat at a computer all day, purchasing little to nothing, talking on a broken cell phone to Al Pacino, who is "coming here to put a bullet in your head!" as one of them graciously informed me before vomiting on the floor one Tuesday morning.

Parinda fired the young girls and hired less flavorful replacements. She changed the lock on the bathroom, which now requires the key attached to a large metal spoon that is kept next to the register: a poop spoon, as it is. The Wi-Fi password changes weekly, many of the electrical outlets have been covered, the dark interior has been painted white, half of the upstairs has been converted into the "office," the music has changed, and prices have been raised. This cup of coffee is four dollars.

Parinda is a very sweet person, just trying to make this place her own, which no one can blame her for. She just finds some of these people frightening and doesn't want them around. She is telling me about the poetry reading the other night. I tell her I write poetry. She says that I should come to a reading. I say "yeah, maybe" and then I say goodbye and get on my bike and cruise through the Abbot Kinney Boulevard merchants festival, which starts later today.

Local artists and vendors are setting up their booths. It looks like old Venice: it's nice to see. A family of cholos arrange hats, shirts, and sweatshirts on a folding table: *HECHO EN VENICE.*

A family of white new-age hippies set up their jewelry booth, daughters helping mom unpack boxes while dad fastens up the structure. Women with crystals and chakras, smelling like a forest in frilly tie-dyed summer dresses.

There she is—Venice Woman—roller-skating down the middle of the blocked-off road, pushing a cart full of supplies, bent forward, happy cleavage, curly hair, bright eyes, sun-kissed and touched with the authentic patient vibe that Venice locals were always known for, and that the transplants are trying to co-opt—to paltry effect.

An old lady wearing all black with thick gray curls of hair sits on a stool with a snarl under a bedazzled hat. Her shirt reads,

You Ruined Venice. She stares me down. She is not being ironic. She wants blood! Just like my old football buddies! Thirty-two groups of Sunday savages—right this very second!—frothing and ready for war.

War, I tell you!

That's how we framed it going in. And that's how it felt. The words they use to get us to buy in. The urgency with which we prepare. The armor we put on. The adrenaline. The danger. The explosion. The violence. The carnage.

Still—it's just twenty-two men on the field. Twenty-two of them and *all of us*: watchers, walkers, eaters, fruit squeezers, poetry readers, constipated sword swallowers, hollow-hearted shit-talkers. We inject our bloodlust into their spines, and they act it all out for us as twenty-two immortal men.

Make that twenty-three!

Gatorade buckets! Brady was right about Dion. He scored twenty points for us. And the McmAnus was delicious. He outscored Matt Prater, 7–2. My two acquisitions were the difference.

In other words, *my* superior managerial skills won *me* the game.

Bunny Sleeve is back!

I'm 1-2.

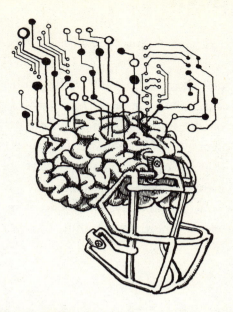

WEEK FOUR

BRAND X

ORANGE COUNTY, CALIFORNIA

Now I'm driving south on the 405 to join a college class for the last hour of a 180-minute lecture on sports marketing. I met Michael, the professor at the University of San Francisco, a few years ago at an event for my book, *Slow Getting Up*, in the Bay Area. He teaches at USF's Orange County campus, too. Tonight's class is discussing branding in professional sports. My experience might be antithetical to what they've been learning: superstars, endorsements, *I'm going to Disneyland!*

I exit the 405 onto the 22. A rising yellow moon leads my

way. The moon is a partially grated wheel of cheese. The moon is a dinosaur eyeball.

I'm early and nervous about interacting with other humans without physically touching them. *Just words?* I park facing a tree and slow-walk toward an open door, my new life echoing through the silent halls of the church that houses this satellite of USF. I stop in the bathroom to wash my sweaty palms and look into my own eyes, just like I always did before a football game.

"This is a new game, buddy. And it doesn't need your body. It needs your *mind*. It needs your mind!"

"Yes, Coach!"

The classroom door is open as I approach. Michael walks outside to greet me, smiling. He is an affable South African, new to the States, and wearing a multicolored scarf thing. He briefs me, says he read my book and that he's excited about the discussion.

"Just finishing up something inside. Come on in and have a seat."

I slide in and sit in the back while Michael wraps up a lesson about tennis player Maria Sharapova's many endorsements. On the overhead screen is a photo of Sharapova swinging a racket. Surrounding her are scores of superimposed logos and brand names. *This* is what branding means: to reach the pinnacle of commercial athletic success, to attain stardom, and then to be tapped by corporations to sell their products.

I had an endorsement deal with the Dairy Farmers of America, during the last year of my career. It was a three-year deal but ended up being for only one year, because I was cut. One Tuesday early in the season I put on my jersey and stood in front of a camera in the locker room of our stadium and read a teleprompter: balanced meals, healthy lifestyles, dairy-heavy, you can do it! Say it with gusto! Say it with aplomb! I'll be your circus boy. Twenty-five thousand dollars for two hours of work and I'll do whatever you want.

Michael tells the students to take a quick break. He told me, via email, to prepare a forty-minute presentation before opening it up for questions. I have prepared nothing. I figured I'd just dive in and chase the sweaty moment up another dark hill.

The students come back to their seats from break. They look at me. I look at them: maybe thirty students. They want to be agents, athletic directors, front office staff, etc. These are good people who love sports, pursuing a career they believe in. Who am I to pull back the curtain?

Michael introduces me. By now I have thought about all of this stuff so often, and written about it so much, that talking about it is easy. Football. Pain. Injuries. Marijuana. Coaches. Doctors. Media. Money. More injuries. Medication. Violence. Girls. Meetings. Practice. The well-intentioned fetuses of the American sports industrial complex are soaking it up.

There are several aspiring agents in this room. I love my old agent. We are still friends. But why do I need an agent? I don't. But I get one because I'm told that I must. If I decide to represent myself, I am eyed with suspicion and treated like a rogue. We wonder why football players are so bad with money. They're locked out of their own negotiations! Two men who have a vested interest in my contract will hammer out the details of my finances in my intentional absence. And the contract will be written in a language that I do not understand. Give me a conclusion and hand me a pen. Sign here.

That's why we go broke. We have no concept of money, and no understanding of the language that explains it. Even now, as I navigate the real world, money matters are foreign to me. When do I ask about money? *How* do I ask about money? How much is fair?

I tell the class about the new book I'm writing. *This* book! It's about fantasy football, I say, and their faces light up. Who plays fantasy football? I ask. Many raise their hands.

"It's interesting," I say. "These guys—their actual bodies, names, faces, *lives*—are the *content* for a multibillion-dollar industry. I think they need to find a way to monetize their fantasy football value better. I think they are being used." I see some puzzled looks.

"Have you guys heard of HIPAA laws? Patient confidentiality? It's illegal for anyone to share your private health information. That's not for other people to know. But football players waive this right by signing a contract. Their private health has become media fodder, and fantasy football is only cementing the need to make it public. That seems unhealthy to me."

That leads to a detailed explanation about NFL health care and my injury history. I tell them I have to sit because of my ankle surgery. Then as I move up and down my battered body—snaps and breaks, tears and incisions—I hear discomfort among the students. Shifting in their seats. This pleases me. They squirm as I tell the story of my hamstring popping off the bone, the surgery and the four-inch scar in my gluteal fold, right next to my McmAnus. They scrunch their foreheads when I tell them about my broken pinkie that was sticking out sideways at an acute angle. They groan when I tell them about my shoulder dislocation. About the athletic trainer with her foot on my chest pulling my arm trying to pop it back in.

As I'm acting out her failed attempt, there's a small commotion a few rows back, tables and chairs rattling. A male student is shaking violently, eyes rolled back in his head, slumping down in his seat, having a seizure. The girl next to him catches him on the way down and lays his head gently on the ground as everyone clears out the chairs and tables around him. It lasts about thirty seconds, then he comes to, well attended to by his classmates.

After about five minutes, they sit him up and he appears fine. "That happens sometimes when I hear medical details," he says, and is ushered out and taken home. Sticks and stones may break my bones, but words can also hurt me.

"Might want to get some weed in you!" I tell him as he leaves. The students laugh but this is not a joke. Recent studies show that marijuana may be an effective anticonvulsant and neuro-protectant and that whatever just happened in his brain could be addressed by cannabis.

After class we go down the street for a beer. When I mentioned fantasy football during class, Michael smiled in the back. This was one of his lessons. Fantasy football has, through the first three weeks of the NFL season, burrowed its way into the collective football conscience with a very aggressive strategy: *total saturation*.

FanDuel and DraftKings, Michael tells me, are being funded by the NFL and ESPN, among other companies, and spent *$25 million* in advertising in week 1 of the season, more than Coke or Nike or any of the rest.

What does that mean for the game I love?

It means that the ship is listing. All hands on dick.

SUNDAY

B-Marsh and the Jets play this morning in London against the reeling Miami Dolphins. The game is at 6:30 a.m. here; 2:30 p.m. at Wembley. B-Marsh has been the most reliable of my heart players over the years. He has set the standard. He is my cornerstone, the player I need on my team for it to gel. He has led Bunny Sleeve in scoring in all three games so far this season. If we all performed like Brandon, we'd be 3-0.

He has taken his good vibes to England for one of the NFL's three London games this year. This is a tough trip for players to make, but the NFL wants to grow the pie and feed it to the world. Shit, every little boy on earth should be marching to football orders. Atten-*tion*!

B-Marsh is hustling out there. I see him working. He wants the ball. Throw it to him! The energy in the building seems low, though. It's a choppy, penalty-heavy game; the restlessness of the fans is coming through the screen. They're not following along.

Europeans are used to a running clock, two forty-five-minute halves: play ball! Maybe we can cut the play clock down and do away with the huddle when we try to implant our game on foreign soil. And while we're at it, we should probably rename it. Armball, anyone? As it is, we are selling rap music at a convalescent home. No matter how many advertising dollars you spend in London, Gertrude is not going to pick up Lil Wayne's new mixtape.

Unless—unless you sample Etta James on the beat.

Whether or not B-Marsh won over the Londoners, I have no idea. But I know he has won over his team, the New York Jets, and his other team, Bunny Sleeve, who, on the heels of his 31.90-point performance, is out to a nice lead in today's battle versus Bruise, aka Breeze. We play music together every Saturday night with a few other friends. It is our jam. We pray to the Jamgod. Many blessings be. During breaks, Breeze and I argue about football and fantasy football because he echoes some of the conventional wisdom rhetoric that I have come to loathe.

What happened shouldn't have happened, wouldn't have happened if the thing that should have happened would have happened! Get it?

I have apparently pleased the fantasy gods. (Jamgod plays basketball with the fantasy gods on Wednesdays.) Despite a weak outing for my man Peyton (9.32), Bunny Sleeve is hopping. Vincent Jackson, my namesake, explodes for 39.70 points.

B-Marsh again is at a solid 24.80, and Pierre Garçon has a great game, too: 22.50 points, jawing incessantly, catching everything, tough as fuck—and it makes me smile. D3, baby! Not many of us out there. But there are some. And they play with their hearts.

Bunny Sleeve wins! We are 2-2.

WEEK FIVE

THE MORTAL MAN

DENVER, COLORADO

" . . . "

"Yep . . . I just got back from California. I go back and forth a lot. No one knows where I am. Helps me write."

" . . . "

"But I struggle with it, you know? Do I maintain my freedom of speech, and with it, a constant separation? Or do I melt in with the goo? And though I may write from inside the goo, I will write only what I believe will be well received by the goo . . . thus I may as well not write at all!"

"..."

"The involved citizen simply can't pull it off. Too many people to offend. Too much judgment. You need separation. Of course, you will suffer for it. You will always suffer! But it bears fruit, this isolation. Don't you think?"

The physical therapy intern doesn't know what to think. He directs me to do one more set of a four-way TheraBand exercise intended to strengthen the muscles in my ankle and reestablish the range of motion. It feels good. I like the scar. I've always found great pleasure in watching my body heal. It is empowering to know that the human body, while injury-prone, is also incredibly strong and resilient. It is always leaning forward, always looking ahead. My body doesn't care about my writing process. My body just wants to heal. My body is a wonderland.

THURSDAY

Today I'm a lion. I look out across the weight room of 24 Hour Fitness and feel powerful. My mind shuts off, gets lost in the movement. Listen to where it hurts, where it roars, where it burns, where it shoots. Listen to the muscles. Listen to the bones. Listen to the music through my headphones. Seventy thousand square feet robust and teeming with eager exercisers on both floors, some of whom are males with exposed nipples.

I propose a no-exposed-nipple policy at all gyms. Steroidouches have a propensity to cut their sleeves in a way that exposes their mammaries. I want to punch them in the neck. Their physique is impressive, but in practical applications of strength, their size becomes a hindrance. Their muscles make them vulnerable. They can't defend themselves unless you morph into a barbell and lay on their chests. They know as much. They are incredibly insecure, which is the point of the steroids.

I shot up HGH after being cut by the Broncos. My career

was ending and my self-worth was crumbling. The HGH didn't help me. I needed something else. I needed someone to tell me what to do, to give me a physical transition plan. But there was and is no one for me out here. Out here I must do it myself.

Find the time to exercise. Meditate on my body. Stretch and realign. Visit specialists. All while trying to move on to a new career and a new life. And still, for no reason at all, I'll wake up some days and can hardly walk. My spine and hips are thrown into catatonia from a whisper, then the long mountain must be climbed again. It takes a constant conscious effort, is the point. An effort that benefits from unclenching what for years stayed clenched. It's time to relax. Time to let go.

But I can't help cracking my knuckles when I hear these fuckboys grunting through another set of curls.

FRIDAY

October 9. In the waiting room to see Dr. Joshua Metzl and everyone is scrolling through iPhones. It reminds me of a story I made up.

Three gazelles were walking through the African prairie. Near a cluster of bushes, they noticed a cell phone lying on the ground. One of them picked it up and started scrolling. "LOL," said the gazelle just as a lion sprang from the bushes and bit down on its throat, ripping it from the spine, blood spraying through the air like a broken fire hydrant. There are lions hunting. Now. Always. And we're making ourselves easy targets.

Ha! *Easy targets?* What's wrong with me? This is a doctor's office, for Christ's sake. Get a hold of yourself. There is nothing urgent about my life now. There is nothing urgent about the moment now: only the need to fracture it.

One bright side of the robotification of America—at least for doctor's offices like this one—is that they can cut down on the magazine subscriptions. *Better Homes & Gardens, Rolling Stone, Time, Newsweek, Golf Digest, Sports Illustrated*—they all appear untouched, spread out like a dusty fan on the end tables. The only worn magazines are *Us Weekly* and *People*.

This is not going well.

Dr. Metzl's assistant calls me in. If her butt could see, we would be gazing deep into each other's eyes as I follow her to the exam room. I'm no longer wearing a walking boot. I took that off three weeks after surgery.

Looks great, Metzl says, when he comes in. Range of motion is excellent for six weeks out. Those little scabs on the scar are a good sign. That means it's getting good blood flow. Ahead of schedule. You should be fine. Start jogging in a month or so.

Ahead of schedule.

No pills.

Marijuana.

Just sayin'.

SUNDAY

Two days ago I was a lion; remember that? Good times! Today I'm a housecat. I was Superman, and today I am No Man. I woke up this morning with a twisted spine. I am the Mortal Man! Shut up! Remember what that Bunny said! *Draft Peyton and write a book about it.* Keep the pen moving and this will all work out.

Today I have *six* Denver Broncos in my starting lineup: Peyton, C.J., Demaryius, McmAnus, B-Marsh2, and their defense. I must reiterate the conceptual foolishness of this design. If the Broncos offense does not score many points, then the Sleeve does not either. We may squeak out a win, but we won't be winning the twenty-five dollars that goes to the high score each week. A more sound strategy would be to space out my players on multiple winning teams, so that one bad day by a team does not sink the ship. But we are not at sea, as it were.

This week, the DraftKings and FanDuelification of the NFL hit a snag as an employee of FanDuel won $350,000 on Draft-Kings. Their sites have identical interfaces and use the same algorithms to determine player worth. Employees have access to algorithmic information that gives them an advantage over online competitors. Now the attorney general is launching an investigation and a class-action suit has been filed by a disgruntled fantasy football player somewhere in Wichita. It appears that a well-crafted insert in a counterterrorism bill from 2006 precludes this whole debacle by excluding fantasy football from online gambling bans, as it's considered a "game of skill." This allows the NFL, whose lobbyists sponsored the bill, to steer NFL gambling money back into their own pocketbooks through companies they invest in.

Oh, NFL—you so crazy.

The NFL and fantasy football make money. But the phrase "make money" is misleading. They don't actually make it. They take it from somewhere else. Where from? Your pocket, mostly. This Wisconsin man who has filed a lawsuit has made taking on FanDuel his cause célèbre. A losing seventy-five-dollar fantasy football bet has launched him into an exhaustive effort to restore his name and recollect his rightful money, which he surely will *not* spend on OxyContin and another losing bet.

MONDAY

Tonight's game carries no weight for the Sleeve. The score has already been settled. Blue Steel gave Bunny Sleeve quite a beat-down. Never lose to Jack! I can just picture him, holding a nice glass of pinot, laughing between sips, not even remembering that he was playing today. "I won? Nice!" And it wasn't even close. And by far my worst performers were the Big 3 Broncos! My season is on shaky ground, people. At 2-3, I have a clogged aorta. I need a stent.

The actual Denver Broncos football team is 5-0. The organism is thriving, but the offense is not the same statistical juggernaut as the year before. They have all-new coaches. New coaches change everything from the previous regime. The players adapt. The players always adapt.

But should they have to?

This brings us to a segment called the Future of Football.

In the Future of Football, the NFL is a professional league in which the players are not just football players. They're involved in game strategy. Involved in the medical process. Involved in their contract negotiations. Involved in media relations. Empowered within the system. Prepared to meet the real world.

The NFL and NFLPA have created more comprehensive programs for former players, mostly having to do with benefits and medical treatment options. But my eyes glaze over when I read the minutia of these surveys, forms, tests, and programs, because I simply do not understand the *language*.

The NFL offers tuition reimbursement for players who want to take college courses in the off-season. I did it twice, both times for writing classes. It was great, but I was very tired from the season. I needed to get away. I needed rest. Most guys feel the same way.

There is also an internship program in which players can be placed in a variety of fields—business, real estate, coaching. But again, it is during vacation, so few bother to sign up. A player's presence is demanded at the facility for roughly three-fourths of the year. If *all* you are doing for 275 days is obeying football commands and speaking football language, you lose the ability to communicate any ideas outside that sphere. You don't solve problems. You don't ask why. You don't read. You don't think. You follow orders.

You speak football.

Funny thing is, the *real world* that football players find so alien, that gives them so much trouble when they're done playing—it's all right there in the same building. Marketing, PR, coaching, IT, athletic training, medicine, management, scouting, groundskeeping, equipment, computer engineering, audiovisual, philanthropy, nonprofit, business: everything that a player might need to prepare him for the *language of life* is happening right on the other side of the locker room wall.

Integrate the building.

WEEK SIX

HOMECOMING

LOS ANGELES, CALIFORNIA

I used to get a large tax refund when I was in the NFL. As a writer, I make far less money and I owe much more in taxes. I'm using the same tax man I used when I played football. I still cannot understand the words he says, nor do I comprehend these tax returns, nor why I owe money, nor how much, nor when.

Tax man has seen my account dwindle steadily over the last five years. He has seen me lose significant chunks in misguided investments made for me by my former financial advisor.

Ponzi-scheme-like commercial real estate company goes

kaboom. My money isn't coming back. It's in someone else's pocket now. Some other athletes got caught up in the same scheme. I suffered a six-figure loss, but my financial advisor never mentioned it, not unless I did, which I didn't, because I *didn't even know it was happening.*

Did he do it on purpose? No. His reckless investments were a product of working with oblivious clientele who never bothered to open their monthly statements.

It wasn't until my career was finally over that I started making sense of it. Then last year my house in Denver flooded while I was out of town. Pipes burst. Fishbowl. As I stood in my basement days later, sifting through mildewed sheets of paper, pulling them apart to dry, some of the only readable documents were a series of urgent letters sent by my financial advisor, telling me that there was an incredible investment opportunity—rock solid—but we had to get on it quick. So here is the form and quick please sign and send it back now!

Yes, of course I'll oblige. I don't have the time or the language skills to decipher this rhetoric anyway. It is in the middle of the season. My body hurts. My brain is shaken. I *trust* you. I sign all documents. All contracts. All bills. I sign anything. Probably should have looked at that one.

So anyway, I got an extension on my taxes and they're due today. That old money ain't coming back. Fuck it. I say good riddance. I do not want your big fancy numbers in my checking account anyway. I want to be free from the burden of unlimited resources.

Enough money to live on is enough money to die on.

I walk in the front door of the Equinox fitness club in L.A. My headphones go on and I'm in church. Follow the body. Listen to the murmurs. Protect what needs protecting. This church is about power and control through pointed movement. This is where I build an animal with the ability to strike. Not only am I making my body strong, I'm training my mind. I am sizing you up.

It doesn't matter who you are. I'm better. I used to tell my Cal Poly friends that I could get open against Deion Sanders and that I could D-up Kobe Bryant on the basketball court. It doesn't matter whether or not it's actually *true*. There's no way to prove any of it. What matters is that I believe it's true. There is more to success than what can be measured.

We obsess over the numbers. We think the numbers make the man. But the numbers don't exist without the numberless hubris of a man who believes he cannot die. I'm the immortal man. The numberless man. I feel the blood moving now. I feel it bubbling now, coming into my fists. They clench around the bar and push away the pain, push away the doubt, push out the indecision with a wordless diatribe—a screed to set the world straight. If only I could bring it back to life:

Total fucking chaos! Give it to me again. Tell me where and when. Give me a task to complete. Let me use my hands!

But all I get is some dweeb with a low hat and a muscle shirt looking around at everyone and talking with the phone cord in his mouth. Do not look at me and laugh, Phone Douche. What is funny here? Nothing is funny.

Motherfucker, nothing is funny!

My workout concludes with a ritual weigh-in and a hand washing and a removal of my headphones, which snaps me out of my jungle trance. The music is a sacrament to bloodshed. I immediately feel more passive. More friendly. The first words I speak come out gravelly as I order a smoothie, then sit down and wait for it. Phone Douche comes up after me and also orders a smoothie, chats up the juice girl. Seems like a nice enough guy, just trying to make his way.

I'm heading home to the Bay Area this weekend for homecoming at my alma mater, Menlo College. Well, they're having "homecoming-like" festivities, but no homecoming football game. The school shut down the football program earlier this year.

But my friend and teammate, a native Hawaiian named Gabe Amey, is being inducted into the Menlo Athletics Hall of Fame tomorrow night, despite the football team no longer existing. We were informed of the program's cancellation on Super Bowl Sunday. The board of directors voted 15–0 to kill it.

I came to Menlo College in 1999 after two years at Cal Poly. And despite "achieving my dreams" in the NFL, those three years at Menlo were the most satisfying football years of my life. Here is an example: On a Tuesday morning in the second week of my third and last season at Menlo, fresh off a victory against the preseason number-one team in the country, I awoke to someone screaming in my hall.

"We're going to *war*! We're going to *war*!"

"Shut up!" I yelled and fell back asleep.

A few minutes later my phone rang. It was Justin, my old high school quarterback, who you will come to know in this story as *Wangs*. Wangs was working in the Chrysler Building in Manhattan.

"Are you watching this?"

"Watching what?"

"Dude, turn on your TV. This shit is crazy. I was standing in the middle of the street and—shit, I gotta go."

You know the rest. The world hasn't been the same since September 11, 2001. No one knew much about Islam or Afghanistan or any of it. The television told us what to think about both, and still does today.

Our quarterback at Menlo, Zamir Amin, was born in Afghanistan in 1979, the year of the Soviet invasion. His parents fled shortly after and settled in Northern California. Zamir grew up as a Bay Area kid in love with football—just like me. And he couldn't find any Division I schools that wanted him— just like me. We lived the same dream at Menlo. Zamir was my *quarterback*. My *guy*. We were connected by invisible wires, communicating telekinetically.

And that Saturday we were scheduled to play Division 2 Humboldt State. But ESPN was reporting that the NFL games were canceled. So were most D1 matchups, mainly because of air travel. But for us it was a road trip.

The athletic departments of Humboldt and Menlo left it up to the players on both teams to decide, which was done swiftly. We knew then what every athlete knows: this game is what we *need*. It will take us away from our grief, away from our fear, away from our mortality—if only for three hours.

Fuck yes, let's play!

After a long bus ride through Northern California, we arrived at our motel. Zamir and I were roommates in room 113. Zamir was number 13 on the field. One of our superstitious coaches asked us if we wanted to move rooms. We laughed and declined.

After meetings that night, Zamir and I lay in our adjacent number 113 beds watching the news: nonstop footage of the attacks, speculation about the attackers. The collective finger was pointed at Afghanistan, at Islam. I didn't know much about either. When you know a man from playing football with him, your knowledge is bigger than his religion or his ethnicity. Bigger than his beliefs and philosophies. You know his soul. It's open for you and yours is open for him. That we were already so familiar made the talking easy that night. Zamir told me about Islam, about its origins and its cornerstone beliefs. He told me about his homeland. He told me about his family. We talked about death. And fell asleep.

The next night, under the lights in Humboldt County, we played the greatest football game *of all time*. We came out very slow and went down early in front of a packed home crowd and a legion of shit-talking roughnecks who came to our sparse bleachers to get in our heads. Interception; interception; fumble; fuck!

We were down 19–0 at halftime.

Our baby-faced offensive coordinator, Dave Muir—only five years older than us—came into the locker room last and flipped out. He pulled the phone off the wall and slammed it to the ground. Kicked over two garbage cans. Called us all pussies. He was frothing at the mouth and his face was violet. He said we were being outclassed. Didn't belong on the same field as them. We fucking sucked!

Dave's tirade had the desired effect. On the first play of the second half, I caught a short hitch versus zone coverage, turned and faced up the corner. Should I go left? Right? Neither! I will cut him in half! I shot myself forward like a missile, put my forehead into his sternum and felt him fold inward. I tasted his heart. It was bitter.

On the next play, Dave called a run. Zamir didn't like what he saw at the line of scrimmage and changed it to a pass, which was intercepted and returned for a touchdown: 26–0. Blood shot out of Dave's ears and he started yelling for Zamir's backup, Chris Smith.

"Smitty! *Smitty!* Where the *fuck* is Smitty?"

Zamir was about to get benched. But then something happened: some celestial mist, some fairy dust, some magic bean. Smitty didn't hear Dave call for him. Instead, Zamir came up behind Dave and tapped him on the shoulder. Dave spun around with crazy eyes. "What?!"

"We will win," said Zamir calmly.

"We will *win*? Ha! Well I fucking *hope so*!"

Dave called off the search for a replacement, and the comeback was on. The game shifted and you could feel it happen. Bang, bang, bang—it started purring, firing—pushing through them like a blade—everything going our way. Touchdown; touchdown; blocked punt: touchdown.

Then we were down eight with one minute left, but they had the ball and we were out of timeouts. All they had to do was run out the clock. They handed off to a fullback and—FUMBLE! Recovered by Menlo College.

Our ball with one minute on the clock. First down: incomplete pass. Second down: illegal procedure penalty. Second and 15: incomplete pass. Third and 15: Zamir heaved it to me down the left sideline. I turned and jumped but it was a bad jump and the play was broken up. The corner and safety celebrated in my face.

Fourth and 15 on our own thirty: forty-five seconds to play, down eight. The Humboldt hooligans behind our bench were in a frenzy. My father sat still with the lens focused on the line of scrimmage. My mother was sitting in the car listening to the game on the radio, too nervous to watch.

Dave sent in the call: "Double right two jet all go." Everyone go deep! I was on the left. So tired! *Hut-hut!* The cornerback got both hands on my chest. I swiped them away and pushed up-field twenty yards and looked back to see a ball of fire spiraling toward me perfectly. I was covered well. They had a safety over the top coming to help. I turned, boxed out the corner, and leaped for the ball. The corner fell and the ball sank into my palms. I closed my fingers and pulled it close to my body, turning up-field just as the safety met my path. He had a clean shot, but all he did was bump into me and try to strip the ball. He was not to have it!

I turned and raced the remaining thirty-five yards into the end zone for a touchdown, the last defender diving at my heels as I skipped across the goal line. Our bench erupted. My roommate, another Hawaiian named Kili, flung the orange thirty-five-yard line marker into the crew of Humboldt mouth-breathers up in the stands. They erupted, too. Security guards had to hold them back from coming on the field and getting their asses kicked. But we still needed the two-point conversion to tie it.

On January 10, 1982, the 49ers' Joe Montana rolled right and threw a high strike to Dwight Clark in the end zone for a touchdown to beat the Cowboys in the NFC Championship. That play was so famous, they named it. It's called The Catch, and it put the 49ers on the mountaintop. Doug Cosbie, our head coach at Menlo the previous year, had a front row seat for that play. He had scored the go-ahead touchdown for the Cowboys moments before. His efforts were squashed by what has become the quintessential West Coast offense short-yardage pass play: sprint right option.

The Catch is a long play, Joe Montana pumping several times before laying it up high for Dwight Clark, who is the second option on the play. He is split wide right. There is a receiver inside of him in the slot. The slot receiver is the primary target. He pushes upfield a few short steps, shakes the man covering him, and breaks toward the front pylon. The quarterback takes the snap, sprints right three steps, and lets the ball fly. It's a bang-bang timing route. The wide receiver is a contingency plan. He takes an outside release in order to spin the corner away from the play and pushes his route to the back of the end zone. Then he bends toward the middle of the field, puts on the brakes, and comes back to the corner of the end zone. That's why Joe held on to the ball so long. He was waiting for Dwight to sell his route into the middle, which he did brilliantly.

Zamir will be Joe Montana. We huddled up for the two-point conversion and Dave sent in the play call. The previous year we played the University of San Diego and it came down to the last play: a two-point conversion, down by two, 39–37. It was the best game of my life statistically: 15 catches for 268 yards and 4 touchdowns, three-for-three passing for 60 yards and one touchdown; and I kicked two extra points. On the last play of the game, we called a "fullback slide" play-action pass and the play got blown up and we lost. I broke down in tears in my father's arms on the field after the game; it's one of the few football games that's ever made me cry. Dave vowed that if he ran into the same scenario, he would call our bread-and-butter play, Joe Montana's bread-and-butter play, and it would be rewarded. He sent in the call: sprint right option.

I lined up in the slot. Eddie Miller lined up outside in Dwight Clark's spot. A defensive back lined up across from me with inside leverage. My chest was heaving. On the snap I engaged him with my hands and pushed away, digging for the near pylon. Zamir took his quick three steps and let it fly. I took two more steps and left my feet, horizontal to the ground. The ball stuck to my fingers. I pulled it into my body as I hit the ground and rolled, holding the ball in the air as I skidded to a stop. Tie ball game. Overtime.

The game was ours to win. Their entire sideline and stands, raucous all game, was silent. It is an eerie and powerful feeling to deflate a stadium like that. And when it happens, you must go for the throat.

We possessed the ball first in overtime and pushed the knife back into the now-exposed neck all the way down to their five-yard line. Dave called sprint right option again. I was well covered this time. But Eddie made like Dwight and found himself alone in the corner of the end zone. Zamir fired a strike. Eddie double-tapped his feet for good measure. Touchdown. The kick was good.

Now all we needed was a defensive stop and we could put it in the books: the greatest game that should have never been played. They attempted passes on first and second downs, both incomplete. I could feel them getting frantic. On third down, my eyes fell on Kili. He was our hard-hitting Hawaiian strong safety: my best friend on the team, my roommate. I took a knee with my helmet in my hand. "Make a play, Kili, make a play, make a play." I stared at the 6 on his chest as the ball was snapped and he dropped into coverage. I watched him watching the quarterback's eyes, sliding to his right. I watched him react to the ball before it was thrown. He broke downhill toward the front pylon, stepped in front of their receiver, and intercepted the pass. Game over.

Seventy-five young men dogpiled on top of Kili. I floated over it, looking down on a delightful mayhem. We jumped around and hugged and laughed and cried. The Humboldt knuckle-draggers slipped out the back door. I found Zamir and we hugged with tears in our eyes: the second time I've cried on a football field. Eventually we made it into the locker room, giggling for the next hour as we showered and changed back into our civilian clothes. Magic just happened; we all knew it. That's why people play this game. That's why I love Menlo Football. And now it is gone.

FRIDAY

MENLO, CALIFORNIA

I arrive early and pop into the bookstore. It's been remodeled. My writing career started here at Menlo, penning articles for the *Menlo Oak*. My first piece was about the exorbitant prices at the bookstore. I look at the price tags on a few textbooks. I did not spark a revolution, apparently.

My book, *Slow Getting Up*, is on display behind the counter. The lady who runs the store has been there for eighteen years.

"You got a new entrance! Looks great in here."

"Thanks! It only took eighteen years."

"No more football merchandise, though, huh?"

"No . . . they made me take it all out of here."

"Really?"

"Yes . . . it was sad. They came in and said 'all of this has to go.' 'All of it?' I said. 'Yes, all of it.'"

"Wow. What did you do with it?"

"Took it to a shelter."

"That's good then . . . I guess. How have sales been since then?"

"Down . . . way down."

A dirty stone ripples to the edges of the pond. From there I make my way across the quiet quad area with green grass and oak trees and check in at the desk. Coming back to Menlo is like re-living a sweet dream. My time here felt guided by a hand that was not my own; the immortal man was permanent; the switch stayed on. The energy was *alive*! And when I see all of these old friends, teammates, teachers, coaches, it all comes back like a wave. And we can all ride it again, buoyed by the mingling memories and familiar touches. But there is a hint of sadness, and a tinge of tension toward those who decided to can the program. Both sides are represented here.

An older alumnus hands me and my buddy Scott Richards *Bring Back Menlo Football* T-shirts. I hang mine from my waist. Gabe's family is here from Hawaii: his wife, Raina, and two kids, Bella and Bear. Five other student-athletes are being inducted as well; volleyball, basketball, golf. It's a happy crowd, all posing for photos. Then the ceremony starts and each new Hall-of-Famer is inducted by a PowerPoint slide show of nostalgic moments: what does it all mean now, as life moves on from these moments?

Whatever it means, we did it together. That's something.

Gabe goes last. The slide show of his football memories reads much like mine; same colors, same smells, same people, same fields, same ball, cutting through the air and charting the move-ment of the same organism. We are brothers. He takes the stage and delivers a polished speech. They said 5–7 minutes. He goes more like fifteen, praising the defunct football program and articulating his frustration with its cancellation. There is a powerful energy in the room, as if everyone is holding their breath. I know I am. Gabe is singing my song.

But instead of belaboring his point, like I probably would, he calmly tells his story. Had it not been for Menlo Football, Gabe and Kili and the rest of the Hawaiians might not have ever made it off that rock in the first place. A diverse community was formed around a common goal, and enriched the entire campus in the process. "The sport of college football is powerful," he repeats one last time, and the ceremony concludes to a roaring applause.

Well done, Gabe.

Afterward we all head to an old locals' spot, the Dutch Goose. I'm sitting at a long wooden bench with initials and names carved in it. There is pizza, and pitchers of light beer, and onion rings, and burgers. I'm talking to Jen Long, my old friend who played volleyball and was an assistant athletic-trainer for our football team. The athletic training budget was not huge. They had to ration tape and hide it from us because we liked to spat our shoes on game day. That means wrap the outside of them in several rolls of tape; mostly for the look of it. Jen would sneak a few rolls of tape out of the training room and hide them in the bushes for me. We are laughing and reliving memories, many of which I have outright forgotten. She is telling me things and it's as if I'm hearing them for the first time. My brain is, I don't know—*rotting*? At least I get a good laugh hearing about the stupid shit we used to do, when there was no tomorrow and no yesterday.

SATURDAY

The next day, as part of the Oaktoberfest lineup, I have a book event in one of the auditoriums. I sit on the stage in a folding chair and read a few passages of *Slow Getting Up*. There are two brothers in the front row, maybe eight and ten years old; Raider fans, pure as rain.

After reading a few pages and yapping for a while, I take questions. That's the fun part. I actually dislike reading from *Slow Getting Up*. I don't know who wrote that shit, but he needs an editor. Carly raises her hand. Carly is an old friend. She is a former college athlete; sports fan, football fan, no nonsense, and no compassion for the million-dollar babies making a living running around on the field while the rest of America toils in the muck for measly salaries and zero excitement.

"Yes, Carly."

"Yeah, you were saying that you think players should be paid more for fantasy football. Don't you think they make enough money already? How can they complain about how much money they are making? You guys are playing the game you love and getting paid well for it."

"Well, it's their performance that is generating the revenue. It's their name, their body, their life. I think they deserve to be compensated for it."

"Yes, but they *are* being compensated. And isn't that what they signed up for? To play football? Isn't that what the contract states?"

"Yes, of course, but the players have to stand up for themselves or they'll get walked all over by the moneymen."

"The moneymen are not keeping money from them, Nate. It's their job to play football. Why should they complain about it?"

"They're not complaining, Carly. They are human beings, that's all. And they're being used."

"Used?"

"It's not all as pretty as it looks. That's all I'm saying."

"How are they being used? They're living the *dream*!"

I look at the two brothers in the front row.

"Yeah, you're right—they're living the dream."

SUNDAY

During breakfast with my mom and dad, I tell them more about the book that I'm writing. My parents are smart football people now because of my long relationship with the sport. My mother knows the game. But fantasy football is foreign to them, or was at first. Now they're starting to get it. My dad saves fantasy football articles for me. Records Sunday morning specials on the DFS quagmire. We talk about the difference between what I'm doing with my friends, and DFS. Money, basically.

"It is *not* gambling!" says the online gambling company. "It's a game of *skill*, in which you bet money on the outcome of sporting events!"

My mother likes the idea of the destination draft, of friends getting together once a year. "Women get together all of the time," she says. "Luncheons, book clubs, sip-and-stitch. But men don't ever see each other. Your dad and every other man in this neighborhood . . . they just don't get together. They don't communicate with their old friends. Isn't that right, Ross?"

"Yeah . . . I guess so. Before I retired, there was the weekly poker game, and we used to play golf. But not anymore."

And I realize between bites of blueberry pancake that fantasy football, the kind I play with my buddies, is more than just a silly game that objectifies NFL players. It is an attempt to stay connected in a life that is tearing us apart. It's a reason to believe in something. It's about friendship. What's at stake?

The Heart of the American Man.

That heart is on full display later this afternoon at Paho's house with my high school friends. Paho has a Revenant beard and long Tarzan hair and moves slowly and deliberately, delivering well-timed one-liners that make his wife swoon from the kitchen as she stirs up a Sunday feast. You know Ryno. Yeah, he's here, too. Also Wangs, my high school QB who I told you about earlier—he lives right down the street. Wangs is lean and light on his toes, with a dark sense of humor that explodes in frequent laughter. Just try to match his enthusiasm: I dare you. You can't. My friends and I: we have particular tastes. Some of them are satisfied by the Sunday glut.

Main ingredient: *football*.

Complimentary ingredients: chili, beer, weed, chips, chicken wings, trucks, gambling apps, diabetes, fantasy football, boner pills, cell phones, insurance claims, vodka, pain pills, shit meds, halftime bets, meat stew, weed, whiskey, more beer, text messages, emails, fantasy scores, one more of everything, then the American Man falls asleep in a pile.

It will take until Friday to feel whole again. Just in time to dive back down.

MONDAY

Mondays are for hangovers.

Bunny Sleeve is up 50 points going into tonight's game between the Eagles and Giants. It appears we'll be victorious, despite another statistically poor performance by old man river, Peyton Manning. This is putting me in a quandary. It's testing my own theory. The Sleeve was buoyed yesterday by another amazing performance by the Broncos defense, which scored 35 points. Bunny Sleeve is winning in similar fashion as the actual Denver Broncos. Winning! That's the name of the game, right?

I will be 3–3 after tonight, and the Broncos are now 6-0.

Undefeated!

But you wouldn't know it in the streets of Denver. Broncos fans are convinced that the sky is soon to fall; more excited about burying Peyton than anointing the entire team. He is being picked apart on screens and microphones, little experts charting his demise. He threw three interceptions yesterday, arming them with more numbers to recite. One interception was returned for a touchdown. The Broncos won anyway.

I imagine these first six games have been quite an experience for Peyton, who is smarter than all of us when it comes to this stuff, but his football etiquette is too refined to speak from the dick. Imagine what an education it would be!

There was a play that happened last night in the Colts-Patriots game that put on full display the sorry state that football finds itself in today. The Colts tried a swinging gate–like formation for a punt attempt on fourth down. They were trying to catch the Patriots off guard and the play went awry. The Colts snapped it to a man who was swarmed by the Patriots and the ball was turned over on downs. The play didn't work. Lots of plays don't work. Plays fail all the time. But the locusts descended on the Colts after the play and haven't stopped yet.

It is okay for a play to fail, but it must fail like *this.* If it does not, everyone needs to be fired. From the top down, every motherfucker who had a hand in this circuslike disgrace-of-a-football-play needs swift retribution. May they never work in this town again for the shame they have brought upon the institution!

WEEK SEVEN

SUNDAY, BORING SUNDAY

SAN FRANCISCO, CALIFORNIA

I am looking for the soul of the 49ers. Where is Jerry? Where is Joe? Tenderloin crackheads don't mistake me for a police officer. They sit in a semicircle and fill the blackened pipe in broad daylight. The Tenderloin is a neighborhood in the middle of San Francisco that reminds me what punishment a human being can sustain and keep on living: toothless mouths, gangrenous warts, elephantiatic genitals and bleeding orifices, crooked spines and jellyfish joints, shuffling across the shit-stained sidewalks with a cigarette smoldering at the lips. They say cigarettes kill, but out here they save lives. A cigarette is a goal.

A cigarette is hope.

The 49ers need a cigarette. They have fallen apart. Consecutive trips to the NFC Championship and a trip to the Super Bowl were not enough to keep the team together. Everyone left. Now they can't win. And they have a brand-new stadium—Levi's—in which to lose football games, and which was funded by the success the exiled 49ers brought them. Levi's Stadium and the Bay Area will be hosting this year's Super Bowl. Levi's Stadium is in Santa Clara, near their practice facility and Great America theme park and close to where I grew up. The Niners may have left San Francisco for good. And being here now, I can see that they're not alone.

My dad was born here in 1929. He packed up his crib and moved to Washington State when he was a baby, but his mother returned to San Francisco late in her life. We called her San Fran Gran and used to come visit. I remember her apartment and the mechanical chair she sat in. I remember the fountain down the street. I remember lying on my stomach on the circular stone and sinking my left arm all the way down into the cold water, reaching for the shiny things on the bottom.

There is culture clash happening between Old San Francisco and New San Francisco. The city is under attack by money. *New money*. Gentrify my love. The nerds are moving in and looking down at the rectangle in their hands, unaware of the magic under their feet.

I'm sitting inside Philz Coffee on the edge of Tenderloin. I write in coffee shops because I enjoy movement around me. It helps me think. It helps me *react*. Prevents me from touching myself. This setting does not discourage all of the patrons, however, from dancing like no one's watching. The bearded lady knows. I've seen her here before. She's wearing a cutoff jean jacket and has a faded rose tattoo on her arm and swipes at a broken iPad all day. Across from her, on a couch, a frail, shaky woman in an oversize windbreaker applies gold lipstick to her eyelashes, fawning into a cracked pocket mirror. She has a busy day ahead of her.

I leave the Loin and walk past the municipal buildings. Human shit under my foot and artisanal coffee in my hand. I'm headed to the Mission District. The Mission is a quintessential Mexican stronghold in San Francisco that was always grimy, artistic, and affordable. Now here comes the money, the good bars and restaurants, and there goes the neighborhood. One-bedroom apartments are more than two thousand dollars a month now. Two-bedroom apartments top four thousand. Houses go on sale and the next day are inundated by thirty offers—five of them in cash, fifty thousand over asking, closing within the week. This is happening everywhere in the district, it seems, but Mission Street, which still feels like Guadalajara. I wait in line at El Farolito for a burrito and drench it in avocado salsa.

This is my San Francisco.

Then I walk heavy-bellied through Dolores Park, a haven for the livers of the moment, the jugglers and laughers, the bangers and jumpers, the strummers and sleepers, the nymphos and creepers. A single bongo drum plays unevenly. A junkie in an oversize navy blue sweat suit dances with the hood pulled over her head. Five years ago, no one pays attention when she drops her pants and touches her toes and shakes her ass and emits a toothless gummy yelp. Because there are thirty more just like her.

Now there's a bunch of people sitting Indian style with fingers on the glass; the ubiquitous San Francisco millennial douche, hoping to record the moment they're repelling.

Later in the day I ride in the back of the tiny Uber car, down 101 to San Francisco International Airport. I'm always sad to leave San Francisco. As the skyline disappears behind us, I look off to the left at Candlestick Park, where I saw my first NFL game. Where I saw Jerry and Joe. Where I saw Terrell Owens and Steve Young beat Green Bay in the last second. Where I caught my first NFL passes, in consecutive plays, in my first pre-season game, wearing the colors of my heroes. Where I— *Shit!*

It's *gone.* Candlestick has been consigned to history. I forgot. Demolished already. Not a single stone remains. I hadn't yet seen its absence. It hurts my stomach.

"Any idea what they're going to build over there where Candlestick was?"

"No . . ." says Sten, the Uber driver.

It smells like weed in his car.

"Probably housing, huh?"

"Yeah . . . I don't know."

"You a Niners fan?"

"Naw, Raiders," he says. "How 'bout you?"

"I grew up with the Niners. But I like the Raiders, too."

He smiles but finds this strange. You're not supposed to like both teams. In elementary school we'd get into fights over the Niners and the Raiders. On the school bus, you either liked the Oakland *Traitors* or the San Francisco *Phony Winos.* So either I'm a traitor or a wino. I want to tell Sten that I'm neither. I'm a warrior! I shed blood on that field! I gave my body for that grass, and now I do not see the colors of the shirts or the logo on the helmets.

I give Sten five stars.

THURSDAY

Bunny Sleeve is 3-3 after loading up on Denver players. Of the eleven starting spots, six have been Broncos. I see this boding well for my chances down the stretch, as the Broncos defense has been carrying the offense. Their offense will improve, and with it, the Sleeve's shot at a three-peat. But here's the shitty thing: the Broncos are on a bye this week. So are the Bears, which feature two of my starters—Alshon Jeffery and Martellus Bennett. That means that *all of my bench players* must start. And we are playing the first-place team: Rocky. He's *undefeated.* I know, right? What a nerd! He loves the 49ers but does not stack *his* team with Niners. He is playing with his head. I must beat him somehow. I need a séance. A rain dance.

I make an offering to the fantasy gods, flush it down the toilet, and then I hit the wire. I need a new kicker and a new quarterback. Since both of my quarterbacks are on a bye, I have to cut one. And since I have only one kicker, I'm going to cut McmAnus and hope he is around after next week. I like him. And I like Jay. But you know how it is.

"Tracy, can you bring in Jay Cutler and Brandon McManus for me?"

"Yes, Mr. Sleeve!"

"And, uh, Tracy?"

"Yes, Mr. Sleeve?"

"Bring me some yerba mate."

Tracy pokes her head in ten minutes later.

"I have Mr. Cutler and Mr. McManus here, sir. And I have your tea."

"*Tea?* Jesus Christ, Tracy! . . . C'mon in, fellas, sorry about that. Have a seat. Look, as you guys know, this is your bye week and you are of *zero* use to me. Nothing personal, you understand, poor foresight on my part . . . but what am I going to do, cut myself? Hahaha!" I laugh loudly and pound the table; the empty Diet Coke can with dip spit in it rattles. I catch it and scrunch my nose. "Ennyway . . ."

Click!

I hit the button and spare them the speech. They'll be back in no time. And maybe back in that chair, too. They are important members of my team. I really believe that. But you know how it goes; it's a *business*. It's funny, they never remember being cut. Or they act like they don't, at least. It's an admirable quality, forgiving your tormentors, bowing to my every demand, no matter how ridiculous. No matter how painful. I marvel at the trust in their eyes as they walk back into my office and sign a new contract, grateful for *my* generosity. Ha! No memory of the fall. No memory of the dogs. No memory of the hell I sent them to.

Only hope. Only football.

Then I have Tracy call in B-Marsh 2 and Andre Ellington, a running back I picked up a few weeks ago in the hopes he'd pan out. Whatever. The two mechanized chairs are part of the same trapdoor. I can drop them out in pairs if I want. You wouldn't believe how expensive they were to install. Got a good deal from FanTraps, though.

"It's like, the best adrenaline rush ever!"

In place of these two fellas, I sign Paul Posluszny, a consonant-rich tackling-machine linebacker from Jacksonville, and the Washington Foreskins team defense, which takes on Tampa Bay at home this week. By cutting Ellington I am able to keep the Denver defense on my team through the bye week. Giving someone else the chance to pick up Denver's D would be a huge mistake. They are carrying Bunny Sleeve. We are 3-3 instead of 1-5 because of the Denver defense.

But if you don't have a consistently lights-out defense, you can always pick up a new defense each week based on the matchup. Look for struggling offenses: the one with the young quarterback and a douchey coach; the one playing on the road; the one with a lot of turnovers. Then choose the defense that they play that week. It seems to work out. But not always!

With McmAnus on the streets, I pick up Justin Tucker from Baltimore, who is kicking lots of field goals. He is on a team that moves the ball well but stalls in the red zone; a team without an established target at wide receiver or tight end: a confused offense.

But I still need a fucking quarterback! And you know what? I'm going to be honest with you. For a second, I actually thought about cutting Peyton. Imagine that! Ha! Nonsense! So I beat that spineless thought upon the neck and head in front of everyone. When it fell to the ground, I stomped on its neck until it stopped moving. And I made sure that everyone else saw it: a show of strength, if you will. This is what happens when you defy the king! This may be "fantasy football" and we may be "playing around" but I'm "not kidding" when I tell you that "I will kill you" if you ever mention cutting Peyton Manning again.

Got it?

In order to remind anyone else who might be getting a little too quantitative with their qualifiers, I pick up Colin Kaepernick from the 49ers as my quarterback for the week. They are playing the Seahawks tonight. On a Thursday night! Thursday night action!

It's like, the best adrenaline rush ever.

Having a shitty week? Of course you are! Want to get some skin in the game? Sure you do! Put a Thursday night player in your lineup and watch your blood pressure soar! It usually doesn't work out, actually, because Thursday games are played by broken men.

But tonight, I have a good feeling about Kappy. He had a solid game last week. He looks fresh. Like he's going to run wild. Like he finally busted through the wall of numbers and is playing the game he knows how to play. I think he will be motivated. I think he will fly. Tonight, we shall test our theories.

Tonight, we'll restore faith in San Francisco. Tonight, we'll kill a few nerds. Tonight, the Sleeve will ride!

FRIDAY

Or not. That didn't quite go according to plan. The Niners got rolled at home against their division rivals: 20–3. Colin Kaepernick scored 4.96 points for the Sleeve.

4.96!

The rest of the 49ers were also off-kilter. The organism is diseased, uninspired. Levi's Stadium is a vacuum-sealed amalgamation of corporate sponsorships. The collective groan that came through my television was less disappointed than termitten. But termites don't eat plastic, so Levi's will stand tall for years to come—a monument to disrespect.

SUNDAY

The NFL is blasting NWA at the nursing home again. Bills versus Jaguars in London today was preceded this week by an American football–themed festival on Regent Street, blocked off for a performance by the Ohio State marching band; then one by the Jags' cheerleaders. Then the star players of each team took to stages to confuse locals with their strange words and sharp jawlines. There were skills competitions set up in the streets with tutorials and televisions and AstroTurf simulation tents and referees with whistles.

Word is that Buffalo fans have traveled well, filling Regent Street with NFL and American pride, shouting Yankee clichés through slurry speech and hot dog breath. There's nothing Europeans like more than Americans taking over their bars. It's the kick-the-door-down approach to selling the game.

You were oppressive! You were lame! We left and started our

own country! We made up our own sport! It's much better than anything you wankers have ever come up with. *American* football. Get it? It's the antidote to your pussiness. Get on board, you stuck-up twats! Come on; give it a try. Throw the ball through the, oh—you can't throw.

"*This* isn't *foot*ball!"

"Yes, it is! Haven't you ever heard of Vince Lombardi?"

"No, mate."

"Joe Montana?"

"No, mate."

"Jerry Rice?"

"No, mate."

"Um . . . Tom Brady?"

"Oh, Gisele, innit?"

"Yes, that's right."

Gisele.

Bunny Sleeve loses in a laugher to Rocky, who goes to 7-0 after the win (*nerd!*). We had too much adversity this week. Leaning too much on the old ting-tong, if you know what I'm saying.

Bunny Sleeve loses.

We are 3-4, in sixth place.

Fuck.

WEEK EIGHT

SIDE EFFECTS

PHOENIX, ARIZONA

A small bag is packed for a trip to Arizona for another cannabis expo. There will be four of us this time: me and Kyle Turley, plus Eben Britton (offensive lineman, six years, newly retired) and Ricky Williams (Heisman winner, ten-year player). The expo's organizers are flying us out and putting us up.

I'm excited to leave my solitary writing bubble. I'm starting to grow hair in strange places and my teeth are getting sharper. My ears are getting pointier, too; I swear it. The other night past midnight I went out for a walk after writing all day and at some point I blacked out and the next morning I woke up on the sidewalk; there were people stepping over me, clothing torn, cuts on my hands, nothing in my pockets, no recollection of what happened.

I see Eben in the terminal with a coffee in his hand. He is a writer, too, and a very large man. He has a relaxed posture and a welcoming demeanor. I met him once, years ago, at a party, before he was even drafted. Now he is freshly retired after a six-year run, similar to mine—mired by injury, frustrated by the dream unfulfilled. This is his first year out of the league. He looks like an active player. Long hair and a beard and arms like cranes. We walk to baggage claim talking about the odd world of legal cannabis and see a driver holding an iPad with our names on it.

"This you guys?"

"Yeah . . . I'm Nate."

"And I'm Eben."

"Okay, guess we're just waiting for Ricky. You know what he looks like?"

"Yeah, it's Ricky Williams."

"*The* Ricky Williams?"

"Yep."

His face changes under his chauffeur's hat, presenting a new crease in his blond mustache. Ricky is famous. Kyle and Ricky played together in New Orleans. Ricky was paraded out as the first pick in the 2001 draft. But four years into an excellent career, he tested positive for marijuana and got kicked out of the league. Nailed to the green cross.

Ricky steps off the downscalator and walks up with a bag over his shoulder, still with the same powerful runner's body. We introduce ourselves and head to the parking garage, where a black SUV is waiting to take us to the Hyatt. There is a cannabis ballot initiative in Arizona that has galvanized the organization of the expo. Legal weed is on the horizon. But we don't know policy. We don't know the laws. We don't know the science. I'm starting to learn about it but what I know best are my own experiences. That is what we can share. Ricky lives in Austin now. Texas's marijuana laws are very strict, Ricky says. You can go to jail for a joint, he says.

"Really? Even in Austin?"

"Yeah . . . there are two statues of stoners in Austin. You'd think they'd be more open to cannabis."

"Who are the statues?"

"Willie Nelson . . . and me."

We check into our rooms and drop our bags. This has the old familiar feeling of a football road trip. Checking into the hotel with my big friends. Here to do a job. It's not quite a football game, but it's something. We meet our contact, Sapphire Blackwood, in the lobby and she leads us one block up and one block over to the Phoenix Convention Center. Ricky is stopped twice on the way by middle-aged men.

"Rickyyyy!"

Aging men, broken men, mortal men: grateful to live in a world where Ricky exists, where they can hook themselves to his belt and ride him through the sky.

Kyle comes outside, happy to see us here in Arizona; he's still using a cane, still overwhelmingly positive. A local television reporter with prominent teeth and powdery makeup wants to conduct an interview outside the convention center. She is blond with red lipstick and smiles embarrassingly as if the assignment is beneath her. She sets up the camera on the tripod and fiddles with the microphone and viewfinder.

"No cameraman?" I ask.

"Nooope! Don't need one. Haha!"

Fiddle, scrunch, fiddle, smile, giggle.

"And . . . here . . . we . . . go . . . so . . . why are you guys here today?"

I start talking and she turns to the camera and grabs the viewfinder again. I forget what I'm talking about, word salad now, and it doesn't matter anyway because the camera is shaking. This footage is unusable.

"When did you start smoking . . . uh . . . mary—uh—cannabis?"

"When did *you*?" I ask.

"I actually have never *done* that before!" she says and her neck scrunches down like a slinky and she laughs up at the sky.

"Never?"

"Nope."

"Why are *you* here?"

"Ha! Good question."

Slinky neck.

After our interviews we go inside and Ricky disappears.

The hangar-size convention center is stuffed with one thousand cannabis-themed booths. This is the burgeoning business of legal cannabis, of which many laws and regulations are yet to be written, and all of them vary from state to state. The laws are vague, still being conceived. There is room at the table for anyone who sounds like they know what they're talking about. *Sounds like.* Remember. Eighty percent of everything people tell you here is bullshit.

Listen for the 20 percent.

Kyle and Eben and I walk through the expo as three trees in a bush forest. I am the smallest tree. Still, I am a tree! There is no actual plant product here at the expo. That's illegal in Arizona. The organizers, as far as I can tell, are a reptilian dude in a baseball hat and Bluetooth and another guy with his shirt tucked in and gel in his air. They are happy to have us here. They offer us things. We decline.

Our booth is in the back far left against the wall. It has a folding table with a football helmet on it, some chairs and a couch sitting on a big roll of AstroTurf, and a GCC banner hanging up behind the table. Gridiron Cannabis Coalition. There's a bar right over there so we get a beer and come back to the booth sipping an IPA. Ganja business cards flying in like ninja stars now.

Within five minutes, we're overwhelmed by festivalgoers eager to meet this week's weed celebrities. Yes, yes, totally, yes. Nate Jackson, yes. Yes. Weed vixens clack across the concrete floor with a dollar and a dream. This is an industry, I'm discovering, that gives hope to the previously marginalized. That gives a business opportunity to a chick with a neck tattoo.

But, wait—or are we all just stoners?

WEDNESDAY

The auditorium adjacent to the expo floor starts to fill up. We are the main attraction today. There are cordless microphones lying in front of each of us. The moderator is a young lawyer named Mike who is working with Kyle and a few others to establish the GCC.

"Dude, I'm fucking *juiced* right now!" Eben whispers to me.
"Me, too."

My heart beats fast. This is game day. But with words!

Mike's first question: What did football mean to us growing up?

We all take turns answering, and, first of all, it's a tricky process speaking into a microphone in front of an audience. There is voice inflection, echo, the odd sound of your voice coming through a speaker, the feeling of being vulnerable and exposed.

What did football mean to me? I don't know. Everything. It was a cause. It was a belief system. It was a dream. It was an actual *thing* flying through the air. Football was *mine*. One of the cool things about writing is that it makes you a better talker. The words I have written came out of my mouth when I was prompted to speak about my football life.

Sitting on the stage with these men, all of whom were first- or second-round draft picks, all of whom are struggling to find their identity outside the game, I feel a sense of community that I haven't felt in years. I wasn't a first-round draft pick. I wasn't drafted at all. None of that matters in the locker room. In there we were all the same. And on this stage, we are the same, too: broken toy soldiers letting down our guard and speaking from the heart about the one thing we all have in common—pain.

Show me your pain. Let's talk about what it did to us, what it's doing to us, and how we feel about it. None of us have any ill will toward anyone in particular. We don't blame anyone. We love the game. The violence was part of the love. Enduring it made us heroes. But questioning it has made us outcasts.

Ricky was kicked out of the league without a bad word ever being said about him by his teammates or coaches. He was charitable, gracious, and kind. He was not out in the streets causing trouble. He was at home, taking his job seriously, medicating with an herb. He was the first pick in the draft, which caused a circus around him. He's shy and sensitive. He got caught up in the system because of a different testing procedure in Miami than in New Orleans.

In the NFL, we got tested for street drugs once a year. Weed is a street drug. It was easy to beat the test because you know when it was coming. But when he got traded to Miami, no one told him that they tested during minicamp. He was surprised when he came into work one May morning and had to piss in the cup. That started his saga with the long arm of NFL law. Ricky was now the NFL poster child for reefer madness propaganda.

So instead of a conversation about how one of earth's best athletes maintains his physical and mental excellence with organic plant matter, we demonize his process and lock him out of the thing he does best in this world.

It feels good to be up here with my brothers, out from underneath the weight of the NFL Shield—the one the NFL implores its former players to protect. There exists a community in waiting of former football players, thousands of us out there, craving the brotherhood but sick of taking bullets for the NFL Shield.

It's no wonder we all disappear when we get cut: reliving the memories is too painful. It's nice to be around people who don't want to know about the Shield. They want to know about us. They ask us how we feel. If it takes weed to do it—fine.

An Asian-American woman with a shaved head has been raising her hand, waiting to be called on. She was at the L.A. expo, too. Someone finally hands her the microphone as she stands and looks me in the eye.

"I want to thank you guys for taking all of those hits to the head when you played football." There are a few chuckles. "Because if you hadn't taken those hits, then started talking about them and what cannabis did for you, I wouldn't be standing here today. I had a bad accident awhile ago and suffered a serious head injury. I couldn't eat, couldn't talk, couldn't think—it wasn't getting any better and I didn't know what to do. I thought I was going to die. It wasn't until I started reading about what you guys have been through that I decided to try cannabis . . . It saved my life. I have my life back. And I want to thank you for all that you're doing."

The panel concludes to a standing ovation.

But, wait—are we all just stoners?

THURSDAY

Brady was right about Dion Lewis. He looks totally unpasteurized out there, shedding tacklers like he's in a video game, stone-faced and silent as he comes to the sideline after a touchdown and plugs himself back into the USB port they have connected to the benches in New England, updating his hard drive with information about the Miami Dolphins' coverages and blitz packages and pass protections. He has a glazed look in his eye. This is what victory looks like. There's nothing quite like winning!

Just give me the hot dog! Show me the baby! And leave me to my porn, my Percocets, and my ESPN—where I am Sex God and Football God. Where I melt into the couch and float through the poppy sky as the one true American Man—the savior in an oversize jersey. The trouble comes when I have to take a shit. You see, these pills have me incredibly constipated. Lucky for me I saw an advertisement for a new medication during the game today—Movantik—that lets me shit while I'm eating OxyContin!

Thanks, Movantik! You make drug addiction comfortable. Now I never have to quit!

FRIDAY

Today Pierre Garçon filed a lawsuit against FanDuel for illegally using his likeness to sell their product. Fuck yes, Pierre! You do Bunny Sleeve proud. The heart beats louder and the head gets smarter. DraftKings struck a deal with the NFLPA—an unknown sum—and FanDuel did not. FanDuel pays about half of NFL teams, another undisclosed amount—but the money doesn't reach the players. Either way, the players would do well to funnel that cash back into their own pockets. The problem is that they have to use a lawyer to do it.

Bon chance, Pierre.

Okay, a few orders of business before this week's matchup. There's a storm brewing in San Francisco, swirling mostly around Kappy and his backup Blaine Gabbert. The first half of the season has been rough on the Niners. Therefore it has been rough on Kappy. His numbers are down. Way down. He can't help us now.

"Tracy! Get me Colin Kaepernick."

"Yes, Mr. Sleeve."

"Oh, and, uh, Tracy?" There's something I've been wanting to tell her.

"Yes, Mr. Sleeve?"

I look at my fingernails: cracked edges, infected hangnails, damaged cuticles.

"Never mind."

Colin walks into my office and sits down. He looks defeated. He may have been crying. I immediately feel very sad for him. All he ever did was want to be the best. Is that so wrong? Now the entire state of California is turning on him. And he's a California kid! He walks in and I give him a thumbs-up with my right hand and a thumbs-down with my left, then I nod at the chair.

"Sit down, bub . . . ain't no love in the heart of the city, eh, Colin? Shit . . . you know that. Look, don't get all down on yourself, all right? They do this to everyone. They used to love your tattoos. Remember that? And the way you'd kiss your guns after a touchdown. Little kids were kissing their biceps on the playground, Kappy! You had that shit by the balls . . . but no one cares about yesterday, bub. They want to see you burn now. And you're not doing yourself any favors, either, man, I mean, Jesus. Look, as much as it feels personal, you gotta remember . . . they ran Joe Montana out of this town. It's not about *you*, okay? It never was about *you*. It's about *them*." I point to my balls and press the button. *Click!*

I didn't know what else to say to the poor bastard. They're eating him alive out there. The moment he started listening to everyone's opinions is the moment he lost it. He trained with

Kurt Warner this off-season, for Christ's sake! Supposedly to learn how to be a pocket passer.

What the fuck is a pocket passer?

Seems to me that a pocket passer is a guy who can't remove himself from the pocket. Which used to be the norm back when the game wasn't full of rocket-armed freaks that run like deer. Colin Kaepernick is one of those freaks. He is an evolved athlete, and he is being hijacked by the conventional wisdom of out-of-shape white dads who tell the world what it means to play *the quarterback position*. I'm sure Kurt is a nice guy, but fuck Kurt Warner; you know what I mean?

"Tracy, get me Jay Cutler, please."

"Yes, Mr. Sleeve."

"Oh, and, uh, Tracy?"

"Yes, Mr. Sleeve?"

"How was your Halloween?"

"It was fine, Mr. Sleeve."

"Did you dress up?"

"I did, Mr. Sleeve."

"As what?"

"As you, Mr. Sleeve."

"Ha! You mean Brad Pitt?"

"I mean a smelly man-child, Mr. Sleeve."

"Ha! You so crazy, Tracy! Just get me Jay, would ya?"

"Yes, Mr. Sleeve."

Jay of course accepts the new contract enthusiastically and thanks me for the opportunity. Welcome back, pal. Let's go win this thing.

MONDAY

November 2. Despite the 6-0 Broncos beating the 6-0 Packers last night in Denver, Bunny Sleeve lost a close one. I started

Jay instead of Peyton, and it ended up being the right move. Jay scored 22.54 to Peyton's 12.60. Peyton understood going in. He took it like a pro. No hard feelings at all, he said, when I called him into my office and told him that Jay was getting the start. Then he did that thing with his lips. You know that thing: the aw-shucks look of pure and humble football virtue. I felt horrible right then. He shook my hand firmly just to rub it in, then marched out of my office and directly onto [Insert Corporate Logo Here] Field, where he looked as crisp as he has all year, helping the Broncos beat the favored Green Bay Packers handily.

7-0.

There's no way to win in the NFL without playing well. There are thirty-two football armies in the NFL, all of them deadly. But the media narrative right now is that the Denver Broncos are 7-0, and until they beat the Packers last night, hadn't even been playing well. A bad 7-0, they say.

I saw an online clip yesterday of my old teammate Rod Smith talking to the current Broncos team at practice this week in advance of the Packers game. Rod was standing in the middle of the circle of football players—right where he feels at home.

Rod became the picture of NFL success by *buying in*. He knows what the NFL did for him and he does his best to relay this to the younger players. He was the guy who taught me how to be a pro. I watched Rod go to work and I copied him. I watched him run routes and copied him. I watched him take notes in meetings and copied him. Not a drop of alcohol, not a hit of weed (*well, sort of*). Never late for a meeting, never forgot a single play on the field. Was reliable in every situation that could arise. He returned punts, he caught third-down passes, he chased down defensive players from ninety yards away to tackle a fumble return on the three-yard line and save the game. Rod did everything that was ever asked of him, and he did it with the knowledge that if it weren't him, it would be someone else in his chair. And he wasn't going to let that happen.

As Rod stood in front of the current Broncos, gray hair around his temples, lopsided shifting from foot to foot, I pictured myself in that circle addressing these young men. What would I say to them? Their football team is 6-0. They have the world by the nipple. They don't know what Rod knows. They don't know what's waiting for them when all of this goes away.

"Y'all are six-and-oh," Rod says, "and y'all aren't even *playing* good!" The team broke into laughter.

"You're *not*!" he continued. "Wait until y'all are *playing* good!"

A football team's collective laughter can mean many things: hilarity, relief, terror, irony. It was hard to tell what their laughter meant through the computer screen. Do they agree? Do they believe that they aren't playing well? Because Rod is echoing the local sentiment, which is that the Denver Broncos are 6-0 despite themselves. They suck! They are a shitty football team that somehow found a way to win their first six games this season.

So were they laughing because they believe that he's right? That they haven't been playing well? If that's the case, then it's coming from inside the building. The Broncos coaches are telling them that. But I don't think that's it. Gary Kubiak is too smart to echo the media narrative and make his players feel shitty for winning. Koob is likely telling them that there are some things to clean up, and that this is a work in progress, but they are playing some damn good football and have beat six damn good football teams because there ain't no shitty teams in the NFL.

So they must be laughing at the irony. It's impossible these days for NFL players not to know what the industry thinks about them. In Denver, the Broncos dominate the airspace. It's what people talk about at work, at home, on TV, on the radio, in line for coffee, on the bus. And the word is that they are not even playing well, because the offensive statistics are askew.

This is how fantasy football infects the mind.

People in Denver think the Broncos stink because their allegiance to the Broncos is killing their personal fantasy teams—just like it's killing mine. And it's hard to enjoy your favorite team winning when your best friend is beating you in the process and sending you all sorts of unseemly texts. Rubbing it in. Laughing in your face. It's not enough for the Broncos to win—to be undefeated. *I* have to win, too. Otherwise this thing doesn't taste as sweet.

The fact is that the Denver Broncos have not lost this season and Gary Kubiak has never lost as the head coach of the Denver Broncos. His NFL life is an original football fantasy. He backed up John Elway for his entire career in Denver. Went to coach the Niners with Mike Shanahan and won a Super Bowl there with Steve Young and Jerry Rice, then came back to Denver with Coach Shanahan and served as his offensive coordinator and won two more Super Bowls coaching his old buddy John Elway. Eventually he got a head-coaching gig in Houston, his hometown. After six years in Houston, he was fired, then he was immediately hired as offensive coordinator in Baltimore, where he cooled out for a year before his dream job opened up and John Elway, the Broncos' VP, hand-picked him to deliver the city another trophy.

There are thirty-one failures every year in the NFL. Gary Kubiak was hired to make sure the Broncos aren't one of them.

So Koob brought his philosophy back to the place that spawned it. But now Peyton is here. And Peyton doesn't do zone runs and keepers and stretch plays and all of the shit that's a staple of Koob's offense. Offensive football in the NFL is mind-numbingly arcane and conceptual. You can tie yourselves into knots trying to decipher these codes and terms. Two offensive planets collided and the result has been seven straight wins to start the season.

The organism is thriving.

But Bunny Sleeve is not. And neither are millions of other constipated Bud Light drinkers who have hitched their fantasy wagons to the Broncos' offense.

For that reason, the Broncos suck!

Bunny Sleeve: 3-5.

Fuck.

WEEK NINE

POCKETS OF LUCK

VENICE, CALIFORNIA

Ryno just called. Myron Zaccheo, our high school coach, died this morning after a five-year fight with pancreatic cancer. Before I ever met Coach, and before I ever put on a helmet, football was just flesh and bone: televised dreams and twilight games in the street. If I played tackle, it was at the park with my friends. Mostly it was in the street playing two-hand touch and watching the 49ers.

My parents wouldn't let me play until high school. I was envious of my middle school friends who played Pop Warner football. I wanted in! That brotherhood. That test. In high school, I got what I wanted. That's when I met the real elements of modern football: metal, plastic, and rubber. I bit down on my mouthpiece and got crushed coming through the A-gap on a dive play during a scrimmage against Andrew Hill High School my freshman year. First carry of my life.

Ding!

Helmet-to-helmet and my light flickers off just long enough to make the spin move I do after contact an act of God. The run gains four yards. I realize as I get back in the huddle that there is a hand at work on the football field that supersedes my own intent. This hand is faster than my conscience. It is stronger and it is smarter.

It is the immortal man.

I had yet to hit puberty then: five foot seven, 130 pounds. I played scout team running back that whole year, getting pummeled every day at practice, learning the feeling of metal face masks smashing on my forearms and hands and ribs; welts and bruises were my new badges; colorful stick marks were collected on our helmets with pride. The more picturesque the array, the more game action you were getting. Mine stayed clean except for Pioneer High School colors—practice hero only—until the last game of the season against Westmont. We were 0-8. Our JV coach, Mark Krail, was a young hothead who couldn't handle the losing. (He is now an unyoung Cool Hand Luke—Myron's prized pupil—who learned how to lose and now only wins.)

"Get in there, Jackson!" he yelled after our starting cornerback blew a coverage.

I jogged onto the field. I remember the feeling of being alone, crouched down in my stance, looking in at the quarterback. I remember the spacing of the players, and the peace I felt in this moment of impending chaos, a moment in which no one outside the lines would be allowed to intervene. I was on my own now.

I remember the dark green grass and the haze that hung over the field and the way their white helmets stuck out. Something shifted in my vision that day, and things haven't looked the same since.

The run play swept around the left side and busted into the secondary, where I closed on the runner and threw myself into his thighs, a blow he avoided easily on his way to a long touchdown. I lay on my back and looked up through my face mask, through the mist and the lights into a completely black sky, starless and waiting for me to get the fuck up. The home crowd cheered.

My football cherry popped.

The next season I grew a few inches and fancied my throwing arm, so I went out for quarterback. New coach, similar result. We were bad. I backed up Wangs all year, starting one game because he injured his hand making a Halloween haunted house. He was ripping off pieces of packing tape from an industrial tape roll when *swiiiishhh*, it slipped from his grip and sliced the webbing of his throwing hand down to the white meat. He needed stitches and had to sit out for our game.

I felt like Joe Montana during warm-ups, but I threw three interceptions that day and we lost. Practice was one thing, but I found that looking past the people coming to kill me was difficult. It wasn't until the fourth quarter of the game that I felt relaxed enough to throw my third pick down the middle, thinking I had an easy touchdown.

Wangs returned the next week and I was back on the bench. Might as well play receiver, I thought; otherwise I won't play at all. I asked my coach and he agreed. The last game of my sophomore year was my first game as a wide receiver, and I caught one pass. It was a hitch and it gained ten yards. My memory of the play was of an accurate ball, a catch, and then being tackled almost immediately.

My father was filming the game, as he did every game. When we got home I watched the footage on our TV, and when it came to my catch, it was as if I were seeing it for the first time. There was a gap in my memory, a moment where my own tape stopped recording.

The ball was actually thrown high. I had to reach up to get it, nearly doing a small hop, then I took off inside to elude the cornerback. As a safety converged on me, I gave him a stutter-step juke to the outside and kept going inside, where I was swarmed and brought down for a ten-yard gain. I watched the play over and over, in awe of that little stutter step that didn't even really work. But how did I do that? I don't remember doing it. Of course I didn't remember.

Before football, I was a lazy athlete. I loved games and competitions, but practice wasn't for me. I viewed practice like I viewed school. It was a system to be thwarted. But football simply did not allow any level of complacency. It requires your full attention. You are under attack. So what will you do, then?

This is where the psychology of the coach builds a winner. So what will you do, then? How will you respond when you get smashed in the face? It's a jarring feeling being hit on the football field. But like a child who falls playing, the reaction of the authority figure determines how the child handles the blow. Pain is part of this. It's part of everything.

Pioneer High School was never a football powerhouse. There are more than twenty high schools in San Jose, and Pioneer is one of the smaller ones. We had only *one* offensive lineman over two hundred pounds: Darryl. We were always the smaller team, in size and numbers. But Coach made it a rallying point.

Your difference is your strength.

It's not the size of the dog in the fight. It's the size of the fight in the dog!

Coach put me in at receiver in game one of my junior year and I caught a touchdown. From then on, catching the football became an obsession. A football game, I learned, is bent toward the will of those playing. Thoughts are actions. Manifest the play in your mind. Believe the ball is coming to you and it will. By the end of the season, Wangs and I were locked in: same wavelength; same interconnectivity.

Throw me the ball; till death do us part.

During the summer before our senior year, I was at a party and the cops showed up. They smelled weed as they walked in and saw this kid named Pepper stashing a pipe under the couch. Pepper had already hid his weed under a different couch, then was putting his pipe elsewhere when he was caught. The cops knew Pepper was their man, but they had nothing on him.

"Where's the grass, son? We know you have it!"

"No I don't."

"Don't lie to us, boy!"

They put us all out in the backyard, then kept pulling Pepper inside—good cop, bad cop—trying to get it out of him. He knew who was holding. We had just been talking about it when the cops came running in. And this time, after Pepper's third interrogation, Officer Buttcock walked outside with a satisfied look and shined his flashlight directly in my face.

"You sure you don't have any marijuana, Nathan? Might want to think *real* hard about your answer this time, kid."

Pepper gave me up. Along with my other two buddies. There were about twenty kids at the party and after Buttcock found what he was looking for, he and a few fellow cops called our parents and invited them to the house to see where their tax money was going.

We were sitting on the floor on one side of the room; our parents were on the other, and in the middle was a glass coffee table with three bags of weed on it. Once Buttcock had the room assembled and quiet, he slow-walked to the coffee table and looked at the three bags of weed. With impressive patience and timing, he reached down, picked one of them up, held it aloft, and said:

"*This . . .* is *Nathan's* marijuana."

My dad's head dropped and he looked at the floor, exhaled, then he looked up and burned a hole straight through me. The officer then introduced the owners of the other two bags, dismissed everyone else, and arrested the three of us for being minors in possession of dirt weed.

The party happened to be at the house of a well-known Pioneer High School booster, who was out of town. We all knew the story wouldn't keep. It would surely make its way to the coaches eventually. My dad wanted me to circumvent that and told me I had to go tell Coach what happened.

"*But!*"

"No buts. Go."

I drove to Pioneer. It was late summer. Two-a-days was starting in a few weeks. I walked into Coach's office terrified. He asked me what's up and I stuttered out my confession. He listened calmly then told me that it was unfortunate that it happened. But he thanked me for telling him. People mess up, he said. It's how they respond that defines them.

So how will you respond, then?

When someone believes in you, you start to believe in yourself.

Thanks, Coach.

THURSDAY

I'm watching ESPN. An earnest roundtable is discussing the crisis at the quarterback position. "Why does everyone *suck* so bad?" they wondered. "These guys are just pa*thetic*!" The media is having a fun go of it. It's funeral season in the NFL. Peyton is this week's it-boy after last week's solid performance against the Packers, but the struggling Andrew Luck is getting a eulogy. The Colts play the Broncos this weekend so it's a perfect time to reduce the complexity of a football game to side-by-side comparisons of the quarterbacks' shlongs.

Peyton Manning and Andrew Luck are the past and present of aw-shucks quarterback football virtue. The put-your-head-down-and-go-to-work guys. The first-to-get-there-and-last-to-leave guys. But the Colts and Luck, favored by some of our little experts to make a Super Bowl run, are floundering. Andrew Luck, the golden boy, has been throwing interceptions and had to miss a game for a bum shoulder. A story emerges that Luck actually has *three broken ribs* that he's been playing through. Not even his teammates know. But now everyone knows, and it has sparked an investigation of the Colts' medical staff and their injury report procedures because in the NFL it is *illegal* to *obey* HIPAA laws. Makes sense, right?

The Detroit Lions buried some bodies today, too. They fired the president and the GM with promises of more to come. "The fans deserve better!" they said. Really? Do they really *deserve* better? Must we uphold this silent pact to pretend that obsessions are virtues? Should you be coddled because you place real-world value on the outcome of an arbitrary contest between transplanted workers?

I think the players deserve better fans, fans who encourage them to be their best, to say what they feel, to stick up for themselves on and off the field, to be given adequate health care, and to protect themselves against predators in wingtips. When the fans start giving a fuck about the person underneath the helmet, then they will deserve a winner. So long as it's a blind allegiance to a corporation, they don't deserve shit.

The Cleveland-Cincinnati game is on. Announcers haven't stopped talking about Johnny Manziel. The scrutiny is too much. Something is going to pop. It seems foolish to make your most prized possession so stagnant, so vulnerable to attack, and to make the movement of the organism completely dependent on his success. And in the event that he is hurt and can't play, the team collapses.

Remember my Jason Witten draft pick? Seemed great at first. The Cowboys were off to a good start. Little experts had them making a Super Bowl run. Then Tony Romo broke his collarbone—as expected—and now they can't win. Why? Is Tony Romo God? Of course he is. But that's not why they can't win. It's not a Tony Romo problem. This is an NFL problem. The quarterback is too valuable. The top is teetering. If I'm a defensive coach, I tell my players to attack the quarterback like rabid dogs. *Hurt* this motherfucker. Break his fucking face. Get him out of the game and we will win. Defenses are barreling down on the pocket with guns blazing.

The pocket! Ha! That's it! There is only one pocket. What happens when you only have one pocket? The bad guys know where you keep your diamonds.

How about two pockets? Three pockets? The center can snap the ball any way he'd like, so long as it goes backward. Who says he can't snap it diagonally to either side based on where they line up? Three quarterbacks behind three smaller lines await a snap. Spread out the responsibility. See how they improvise.

Every skill position player on offense has to know how to throw, and be ready to throw from all angles. With three potential pockets, the spacing of eligible receivers would change, as would the angle of pursuit for the defense. Defenses benefit from the predictability of offensive football. They know what is coming, so their rules and language stay rigid, fixed on five down linemen, toe to toe, with a downhill-run blocking game and pocket passing game. Numbering systems and codes are developed and taught to the defense based on predictable offensive formations.

So who will shake up the Etch A Sketch? There is a formation that will do it. It will confuse defenses and collapse zone coverages. It will create new holes and new angles as the action bursts not from one cluster of players but from two or three. Who do we cover? Where do we run?

Different pockets would also allow players to rest if the play went the opposite way. Typically that's blasphemy in football. You don't take a play off. Ever. You compete. You chase down defensive players from across the field to get in position in case a run breaks into the secondary and you can be there to make a block. If you don't run hard and a defensive back makes a touchdown-saving tackle then you get called out in meetings and your job is threatened in front of your peers. You go as hard as you can on every play, all play long. That is the football way.

But is it the most effective way?

What happens if half the team simply does not move when the ball is snapped? The half that is covering them up will not move, either. You have just removed half of their team. Neutralize their stronger half and you gain an advantage. Confuse them with changing speed and you gain an advantage. Flummox them with new formations and you gain an advantage. Allow your players to improvise and you gain an advantage. Otherwise you are working from the same tired template, adhering to the same rules because "everyone does it."

Forgive my Future of Football pipe dreams, people. I'm such a kidder: "a California hippy fag," as one of my old teammates eloquently put it when we were arguing about politics in the locker room. They say you should avoid politics in the locker room. Too distracting. Stick to football-speak. But Barack Obama was running for president and a lot of the black guys on my team were stoked. So was I. "Nate, you know you ain't white." I got that a lot. Nate Jackson. Football player. Rapper. I get it. But I was white. I still am. And none of that really mattered in the locker room. It was how you carried yourself, what you did every day, how you handled locker room situations that got testy or violent or whatever. How you handled your business on the field. You don't want us to talk politics? Why? We are the perfect people to talk politics. We prove that "politics" don't matter when someone is hitting you in the face.

Don't hold my optimism against me here, folks, but I'm fairly sure that Bunny Sleeve is about to go on a run. It's a good thing we got rid of old Kappy because the vultures have descended on him. He was benched this week. Blaine Gabbert will start. It is inadvisable to start Blaine Gabbert for your fantasy squad. Smoking meth is also inadvisable. People still do it. People are doing it right this very second.

The Niners coach, Jim Tomsula (or is it Tom Jimsula?), says Kappy just needs to take a few steps back and chill. Everyone else in the Bay Area is yelling about it, too, but their voices are indistinguishable from the rest. Kappy is the fall guy. The Niners are shit because they lost everyone. They lost their psychotic, win-at-all-costs coach, lots of starters, Candlestick Park, and San Francisco. It might say "San Francisco" on some logo but there ain't no *city* in the Niners anymore. The only one who stuck around was Kappy.

Newsflash, assholes: the quarterback is not enough.

The irony here is that Bunny Sleeve's starting lineup is pretty set right now; all except for my quarterback. Here's what it looks like:

WR: Brandon Marshall
WR: Demaryius Thomas

RB: Dion Lewis
RB: C. J. Anderson
TE: Martellus Bennett
W/R/T: Alshon Jeffery
W/R/T: Pierre Garçon
K: McmAnus
DEFENSE: Broncos
DEFENSIVE PLAYER: B-Marsh 2

My only point of contention is this: Jay or Peyton? If only they could both be on the field, each behind a pocket of three: imagine what the world would be! But I must choose: Jay in San Diego, where he struggles? Or Peyton in Indianapolis, where his career began? Jesus returns to Bethlehem to find another well-meaning dude nailed to the cross—Andrew Luck. To compound the story, Peyton is 278 yards short of the all-time passing yards record, held by Brett Favre, who has agreed to promotional advertisements for the game.

So who will it be? Jay or Peyton? I do not know yet. I need to shake things up before I have my answer. I need to stir the pot. Bunny needs a shot of life!

"Tracy!"

"Yes, Mr. Sleeve?"

"Get Vincent Jackson in here."

"Yes, Mr. Sleeve."

"And Tracy?"

"Yes, Mr. Sleeve?"

"Tell him to bring his playbook."

Time to trim some fat. Vincent has been unproductive lately. Yeah, he's had a few good games. Like three weeks ago! We won't stand for mediocrity. A coach must never allow it. If you want to make pancakes, you have to kill a few chickens. Vincent walks in holding his book. I put my toothpick behind my ear, nod for him to sit down, and reach out for his playbook. He hands it to me, trembling. He knows what's next. Shit, everyone knows what's next by now. If it weren't him, it would be someone else. Someone who is ready to make the ultimate sacrifice for his sport, for his team, and for his fans. The ones who matter. The ones who get it. The ones who will always be there, waiting for him to fall, ready to destroy him. I put my hand under my desk, slowly, and grab the new playbook that I prepared for Vincent, then reach across the desk and hand him his new life. He gulps and grabs it.

"That one was getting old, Vinny. This here's the updated version. Oh, and I left you a little something in the sleeve. A bonus for all that you've done. It's exactly how much I think you've been worth so far this season. Not a penny more! Now go on, get out of here. You've got meetings. And don't fall asleep! I'll be watching."

SATURDAY

Now I'm back upstairs at Self Espresso, drinking filtered drugs and eating a donut on the sly. They don't sell donuts here, and there is a "No Outside Food Allowed" sign on the wall, another keep-out-the-riffraff gambit. Am I, then, riffraff?

This is a $3.75 donut! This is an *Abbot Kinney Street* donut. (Abbot Kinney is a fancy street where the people look like mannequins.) An artisanal donut. A donut presented on a plate. A fucking irritating but delicious donut. A buttermilk old-fashioned donut. This is not a riffraff's donut. This is a stand-in-line-then-place-your-order-and-wait donut. A new-money donut.

Gentrodonut: displayed like a diamond ring at a jewelry store. Behind each donut in the all-white case is a handwritten note card stating its flavor. I escaped without putting my foot through the glass, and now here I am, mulling over my quarterback decision for tomorrow: Jay or Peyton, Peyton or Jay? I still don't know.

But I do have a few DFS tidbits to relate. FanDuel and DraftKings saw revenues *jump* after the insider trading "scandal" that exposed it as a racket. So we know what kind of customers we are dealing with.

Also, seven out of ten of ESPN's top-viewed articles of the month were fantasy football related. Basically, the articles are just recommendations on who to look for on the waiver wire. Little experts are making ESPN and the NFL big money. Money makes money for those who have money. Money has heels. Heels dig in.

Fantasy football is here to stay.

Ahhh.
Finishing a good writing session is like waking up from a dream. I feel refreshed as I reenter the atmosphere.

I close my laptop and shake out my hair. Bats fly out. I get on my bike and ride from Self Espresso to Venice Beach, which is a few blocks away, and watch street hoops. My ankle is improving daily. I hope to be able to play basketball again, but I do not know if I ever will. This thought torments me. I need to run and jump! I need to land an elbow on someone's neck. I need to hurt someone! And I will again, God willing. Until then, I like to watch this pickup game for a few minutes when I ride past. It is one of the most famous pickup courts on earth, and not necessarily for the quality of play, but for the ambience.

The courts are lined with unswaying palm trees. Stone benches and green grass patches surround the courts. Skateboard tails clack in an adjacent skate park. Beyond that are street dancers attracting meat circles around the electric bugaloo and a bucket. And on the main court, ten shirtless sweaty ball hogs toss up prayers and call false fouls.

"Yeah, mother*fucka*! That's what I told you! That's what I told you!" The real-life Willie Mays Hayes screams as if starring in a theatrical performance of *Venice Beach Basketball*. It's game point. If Willie scores, his team wins. He has the ball at the top of the key. A crowd of tourists watches on cement bleachers. Junkies eye their bags. Willie dribbles, dribbles, zigs right and zags left, well defended. He runs toward a double team and before he makes contact, slips and falls on his ass.

The defender reaches for the ball and a tussle ensues. Someone yells, "First!" Finally the defender gains control of the ball from Willie and takes it coast to coast for an uncontested layup.

"*My* ball, nigga!" yells Willie from flat on his ass. "*My* ball, nigga! *My* ball, nigga! Don't go changing the rules *now*, nigga! Don't go changing the rules *now*!" He repeats this incantation as he jumps up and stomps in a big circle, covering the entire stage. After several minutes, his opponents relent and give Othello possession.

"Watch that cheatin'-ass nigga over there!" yells his opponent. "He gonna steal the game."

Willie gets the inbound, faces up the hoop, takes one dribble, and launches a thirty-footer.

Swish.

Game over.

Willie stomps the court again, screaming his newly minted sermon. People shake their heads while he circles around the bathrooms—"Get off my *court*, nigga!"—and finally returns to the playing surface, where the winner stays on.

There is no justice in sport.

Continuing along the path, I see my neighbor Brian and his wife walking their two pit bulls on the grassy island. I stop and they jump on me. The dogs, I mean. "They know you, dude!" Brian says. I told Brian about this book idea a few weeks ago and he nearly choked. "Dude! *Dude!* I used to host a fantasy football radio show back in the day. I wrote two books about it. We need to talk, dude." I pet his dogs and he introduces me to his wife. She is wearing large sunglasses and is on the phone.

"Dude, so you're really writing that book about fantasy football?"

"Yeah."

"The thing is that perfect information was attainable back in the day when you researched it yourself. But now anyone can play. All of these sites do all the research for you. Shit, a *computer* beat me last week . . . *seriously*! Someone who autodrafted beat me. It takes the art out of it, man. Guys don't even follow their teams and they can still win. It's all fucked up now."

"What do you do if someone forgets to set their lineup?"

"We send a note to the commissioner and he takes care of it. Gotta have everyone's lineup set, dude. Plus trades and everything. I'm on the trade committee in a few of my leagues."

"Trade committee?"

"Oh yeah, dude, gotta maintain the integrity of the league." I laugh. "It's *true*, dude! I have to protect everyone from stupid trades that undermine the integrity of the whole league. Like, okay, what happens if two teams want to trade Ronnie Hillman, who is, whatever, for Johnny Manziel?"

"What do you mean?"

"Well, do I let that trade go through? Ronnie Hillman is almost a starter and Johnny doesn't even really play."

"Maybe someone likes Johnny Manziel and wants him on their team."

"Ehhh."

"No? Maybe they're just choosing with their hearts."

"No, no, no—never do that! Gotta go with your head, dude."
He taps his temple.

"How many leagues are you in?"

"Twelve."

"Twelve?"

"Thirteen," says his wife, then turns back to her phone.

"Yeah, I guess it's thirteen."

WEEK TEN

BLANK SCREEN

VENICE, CALIFORNIA

Bunny Sleeve is 3-6 and on life support. The Broncos lost handily in Indianapolis, in all phases, which sunk my ship. The Sleeve would have lost with either Jay or Peyton. This is about the time in the season when panic sets in. Jobs start to feel tentative. People start looking at you funny in the halls.

I need a plan. I sit down at my desk. The room feels smaller today. Why are the blinds like that? I left them all the way down. That's for sure. I pick up a stack of pages and look at them in my hand. These have not helped. I flick them across my office backhand and they spread in the air like a flock of doves, then fall dead to the carpet.

"*Tracy!* Jesus H. Cranberry!"

"Yes, Mr. Sleeve?"

"Call me 'Coach' from now on, okay?"

"Okay, Coach."

"Help me clean up these papers, would ya?"

"Yes, Coach."

She crouches down and her feet shift a little in her brown flats as she reaches out collecting pages. Her body moves and, it's just, I don't know how to tell her that—you know, that I appreciate her. Not just for the work she does, but for being here, you know? She is so strong. Sometimes I think that if it weren't for Tracy, I'd have lost the will to live. She stands up with the papers held against her chest and puts them down on the edge of my desk.

"Thanks, Tracy."

"You're welcome, Coach."

"Oh, and, uh, Tracy?"

"Yes, Coach."

"Send in Dion Lewis."

Unfortunately for Bunny Sleeve, Dion tore his ACL in the game. It's over for him. He walks into the room on crutches, his face blank.

"Dion, my guy! How's that leg?"

"It malfunctioned, sir. I couldn't perform my function, sir. I made a mistake, sir. I have let down the team, sir."

"Whoaaa! Jeez, bub! Don't be so hard on yourself. Who's been pumping you full of this? You gave it your all out there! I know you did. Hell, you did a heck of a job for us while you were healthy. No matter what happens from here on out, you'll always have that game film. No one can take that away from you. You remember that, okay? Look, I wanted to go over your

X-ray and MRI reports with you so you know what's going on with your knee, but you know what?"

Click!

What do we care, right?

He hits the dungeon floor like a cybernetic organism. His crutches land next to him with a clinkety-clink and the dogs clamp down with hungry teeth onto Dion's bio-injectable metal-tissue support-cell armor, part of the Patriots' new nutrition plan. The dogs don't like the taste.

I am hitting the waiver wire for Bills rookie running back Karlos Williams again. I've been watching him all year, waiting for LeSean McCoy to get hurt. C'mon, LeSean! Break already! Featured running backs eventually get hurt, and their backup falls into that role and has some huge games. Next man up. Thanks to violated HIPAA laws, I know that LeSean has been fighting a shoulder injury, and I hope he is badly injured, much worse than reported, and I hope to get Karlos back on Bunny, where he belongs.

We need help at running back and we need it now!

Against the Colts Peyton ended up three yards short of Brett Favre's record. They had the champagne ready. The cannons loaded. The midgets were hiding in the cakes. The hookers were naked in the limos. Everything was ready. All we need is a few more numbers! C'mon, Peyton! Keep coming! Certainly, records are part of sports, and this record is one worth keeping. But this has become a common refrain in the world of sports:

For the first time ever!

Just because we measure it, that doesn't make it novel. It's physics. The farther back you pull the slingshot, the harder it will shoot. Players are the stones. As the Broncos and Colts game unfolded, the pregame narrative changed in real time. Peyton struggled in the Dome, and Andrew Luck, who was, by media accounts, a leper going into the game, played very well and led his team on multiple tough scoring drives with physical runs and accurate downfield throws. "Well, *this* is the Andrew Luck that we were *hoping* we'd see!"

Why are you holding shovels, then?

After the win, Andrew Luck was held aloft long enough to make today's news of his lacerated spleen another tear-jerker for the aw-shucks crowd, who hate to see a guy like that go down in the middle of the season right when he was starting to get it clicking again. Your heart goes out to Andrew for all of the—

Click!

Save it, Trey. But I wonder if the sharp edges of Luck's three broken ribs had anything to do with the laceration of his spleen?

Peyton's proximity to Favre's record makes it a guarantee he'll get it this week. The game is Sunday in Denver against the Chiefs, and I will be in attendance with a freelance writer called Mr. Green.

Mr. Green got someone to buy tickets and pay his way to Colorado so we can talk about ganja. I obliged his request. I'd like to see the Sleeve perform in person, and see how bad the Broncos suck, and court some old demons, and have something to do, something to *write about*. I'm doing this for *you*, dear reader!

NFL wisdom is dispensed weekly. We don't learn the nuance because we are fed the numbers, which we gorge on.

Here is the real wisdom: *kill the narrative.* That's how you win games in the actual NFL. The narrative is the fantasy. And the fantasy is a lie.

Kill it!

I need to kill some narratives of my own.

One is that I am a victim. Let me explain. My first book received some Hollywood interest, enough to make me think that my six seasons in the NFL would be a good template for a television show following the rise and fall of a professional football career. I was working on a pilot script and talking to a few producers when I was contacted by a writer/director named Peter Landesman, or as we'll call him, Hollydouche—Guy Hollydouche. He was working on a script about concussions and head injuries in the NFL and wanted to talk.

We met at a restaurant. He was wearing a deep V-neck shirt, had plentiful woven jewelry and an improbable tan. He praised my book. So authentic! So raw! You've got a real gift! He wanted me on board for the film, he said. Sony was green-lighting the script and Will Smith would star. Sony would option my book. I would work on the film, be in it even, be there on set, in the editing room, get a feel for how these things are done—then eighteen months later when the movie was out, Guy would help me write my TV show. We'd do it together! We'd be partners in this thing. He had never done that before but we'd figure it out!

"Wow! Cool!"

My new Hollywood agent at CAA, presented to me by my literary agent in New York, told me that this was legit. It was happening, and contract negotiations started. I shelved my own television project as Guy pumped me for information about the NFL. I told him that I wrote twice as much material as what ended up in my book.

"Send it to me!" he said. "Send me everything you have!"

Skeptical of his flippant declarations, I visited him again to be assured that putting my project on hold and coming aboard his was the correct thing to do. I sat at a huge table in a conference room at the studio and he walked in five minutes later with a painted-on smile and high-arching eyebrows. He stroked my ego, told me what they were working on, how I could help, what legal snags they were running into, and what the schedule was.

A month later, at Guy's request, I went into the studio, owned by the film's wealthy producer, signed a nondisclosure agreement, and read the script. The script was good. Well written and sad. I don't know. It was the first script I had ever read. There were some anachronisms that I caught, and there was some football dialogue that came out very writerly—"C'mon, man! You pulled an *audible* on me!" Also the script never mentioned CTE, which is the name of the disease that the story is focused on. I gave an assistant producer my notes while her little dog ran around the office jingling its stupid collar. I left feeling part of the project, despite the fact that contract negotiations had stalled—some discrepancies in the fine print; standard logjams. Carry on! We'll get this worked out!

Filming was to start in late October in Pittsburgh. In September, Guy connected me with Freddy Football, who was organizing the football scenes and said I could be in them if I wanted. This excited me very much. I get to suit up again? Smack it around a bit? Play catch? Yes! I started training for it: lifting hard at the gym, running on the grass in cleats, getting ready to play some *football.* This was a very bad idea, in hindsight. My body is and was wrecked. I have no business playing tackle football ever again. But there was something stronger at work, and I was *all in.*

But a week before shooting commenced, I still had no contract. My agent at CAA had said "any day now" every day for the last four months. But now it was time to shoot. And people don't start shooting before getting paid. As we waited for the next response from Sony, I reached out to Guy and Freddy, because, despite all of the planning, no one had contacted me with flight information or lodging or anything logistical. The movie sounds great. I'm very excited. Can't wait to suit up one last time. But could someone tell me where to go? Where I'm staying? Who is going to pick me up? *Hello?* Is this microphone on? Guess not.

Radio silence.

Repeated calls, emails, and texts went unreturned. Guy fell

off the map. So did Freddy. I called my agent. "What?" he said. "This never happens!" But the filming commenced a few days later without me. Finally an unfamiliar assistant producer wrote me an email and said that there was some kind of a mix-up, that they didn't have it in their budget to bring me out there and that they had all of the spots filled. The film comes out on Christmas Day and is called *Concussion*.

"*Concussion?*"

"It's the hard-*c* sound," my agent said. "Hard-*c* sells more tickets. It's appealing to the ear."

The concussion topic is timely and important. It affects me and it affects my friends. It affects current and former players; wives, brothers, children, parents. But it does not affect Guy Hollydouche or Freddy Football or anyone else in the hard-*c* crowd. For them, it affects their IMDb page and their ability to get last-minute reservations at Spago, or wherever the fuck.

C*oncussion* opens on Christmas and Sony is having several screenings of the film in advance of its release. "You'll be getting credit as a consultant," my agent wrote me. "Let me know if you want to go to any of the screenings and I'll arrange to put you on the list."

Time to grow up, Nate. You're not a victim. I responded favorably to the offer. The screening I chose is tomorrow morning at ten on the Sony lot in Jimmy Stewart 23. I shall go and I shall be the model of benevolence and forgiveness. And if Guy is there then I'll spring in the air like a panther and land on him with all of my weight, pinning him to the ground, and smashing down with a double hammer fist until I feel the bones in his face break, snap, and crack like bloody eggshells while the SAG members stand and watch.

WEDNESDAY

I park in the Sony lot and walk to Jimmy Stewart 23—a one-hundred-seat screening room, which is mostly empty—and sit in the third row. Maybe twenty people are here. Guy is not one of them. Seems like press. The film starts and it is good. It's surreal to watch it, to see how the shots came together, how it went from page to screen. I already read the script. I know how it goes. There is nothing surprising; it sticks faithfully to the story. Guy is a journalist. He took some heat a few months ago after the Sony hack. The media interpreted the leaked documents as Guy folding to NFL pressure. Didn't seem that way to me. I was, in fact, surprised at the amount of NFL footage and logos and team references that were made. I thought the NFL would prohibit that.

The story is about a Nigerian doctor—Bennet Omalu—who discovered a brain disease in former NFL players. The disease is called chronic traumatic encephalopathy (CTE). The conclusion of the film is this: *football kills the brain.*

Now talk amongst yourselves.

The implications are plain. I cringed a few times, felt a shock in my cortex. Sometimes my football life feels like another life altogether. It wasn't me out there. I don't know who that was or how I trained myself to do that: to be the attacker, to use my head as a weapon. But using the head as a weapon is the only way to survive a life of football, and you get used to it.

Put a hat on him.

Stick your head in there.

Knock him out.

Light him up.

The game is played with violence and strength, force and aggression. It's about the *final blow.* That we have convinced ourselves that it can be made safe speaks to the power the game has over us. It represents something that we consider valuable and instructive, and therefore worth keeping around. We are not giving it up. Fine. But let's not play double Dutch with uncooked spaghetti.

Football kills the brain. Yes, this kind of makes sense when you think about it. But does football have to kill the brain? No. But as long as those who control the game don't get hit, and the rules and medicine stay the same, the game won't change.

Until then, what's the safest way to get hit by a truck?

The only thing that disappointed me about *Concussion* was the use of English actors for hardened American football player roles, like Dave Duerson's character. You can't throw, bloke. I can tell by looking at you.

One of my former Niner teammates, Matt Willig, has a role in *Concussion*. He plays Justin Strzelczyk, a former Steelers lineman who died a violent death after becoming demented. Matt is a huge man. Scary man. Nice man. And an actor man!

To me, the most visceral part of *Concussion* is not the power struggle between Omalu and the NFL, but the depiction of the downward-spiraling former football player that has become the all-too-common cliché. Every former player in the film dies a horrible death, either by suicide or something close to it. The implication here is that they couldn't help it, that football drove them mad. So what is left to do but die? It's a fatalist look at the plight of the former player. And it's unhealthy to take it as the final word.

Remember when Rocky and Apollo Creed land crosses simultaneously at the end of *Rocky III*? *Concussion* builds to a similar climax. Two high school players run toward each other from a distance and it cuts away right before impact. Right before the damage. Right before the dinner bell.

The credits roll. Ha! There I am. Look, Ma! I'm Consultant-Douche.

THURSDAY

Meanwhile, FanDuel and DraftKings are swimming in money like Scrooge McDuck, but like Hank Williams said, "Mo money, mo problems." After already having been kicked out of Nevada by the gaming commission, this week they were given the same treatment by the attorney general of New York, who told them to scram. Cease and desist. But they intend to fight this one and have hired some other prominent nerd to defend them. New Yorkers apparently play daily fantasy more than most.

It's like, the best adrenaline rush ever!

Right now I'm on a small American Eagle airplane, headed to Denver to watch the Broncos play the Chiefs on Sunday. I just sat down and already cannot get comfortable. I want some Thursday night action to lift my spirits. As the stewardess is explaining the complicated seat belt locking process, I'm frantically retooling my lineup to make the moment I turn my phone on after landing a more powerful one. I want to have a numbergasm right here in 12D. Put the barf bag to use. I insert Karlos Williams in my starting lineup, joining B-Marsh. Double action! My opponent, Skone, is starting LeSean McCoy, whom Karlos is backing up. It's a gamble.

It's like, the best adrenaline rush ever!

Wheels up and I sit back and picture all of the touchdowns Karlos and B-Marsh are scoring, and I picture LeSean McCoy sustaining some awful, bone-snapping injury. I chuckle as they cart him off and he gives a thumbs-up to the crowd. Godspeed, LeSean! Get some rest! The man next to me is watching a spaghetti western on his phone and the two strangers behind me greeted each other upon sitting and haven't shut up since. "Oh, really? Kansas? Closetry? How *interesting*!"

Mercifully we land and I turn on my phone in hot anticipation. It's like the best adrenaline rush ever. It's like . . . fuck! B-

Marsh and Karlos have totaled 29 points, as has LeSean McCoy on his own. Looks like his shoulder held up after all. Bummer!

FRIDAY

Today there was a pro–fantasy football protest outside the attorney general's office in New York, apparently staged by DraftKings and/or FanDuel, but it was also attended by daily fantasy devotees who wanted their voices heard. Reportedly, all in attendance were constipated.

SUNDAY

Game day, bitches! Today I will revisit my NFL experience from the nosebleeds with Mr. Green, hoping to pick my brain clean. I park at a church (twenty dollars) and walk to the stadium and find my buddy Jake Plummer tailgating in the parking lot. Jake is the Broncos' third-most-famous quarterback ever. All three will be here today. Jake's hair is parted in the middle and floppy. He chuckles often and his hands hang open as if ready to grip the football and hit someone down the middle on a skinny post. He is doing the coin toss at today's game. It's funny, they're hard on you when you play—especially the quarterback—but they love you when you retire.

The memory is sweet. Now is salty.

Now is an acquired taste.

Mr. Green's photographer, Lenny, shows up first and takes me through a series of embarrassing photos at the bottom of a packed stairway. Broncos fans file past us holding beers and yelling. Mr. Green wanted to shoot video, too. Make this a big thing. I nixed that and agreed to still photos instead, which I'm now regretting, having already spent years as a circus monkey.

But simply by talking about cannabis, I have made myself

an attractive proposition to guys like Mr. Green, who want the inside scoop and a check from a website willing to pay for original content.

"NFL guy smokes pot and is willing to talk about it" is original content. "Wait! You like weed, *too*?" Standing ovation. But I suppose we both have an agenda here. I am also writing about today. Mr. Green just doesn't know it.

He walks up and introduces himself, straight from the airport; he is a short, affable fella with a beard and a baseball cap. I hand him a beer, Mama's Little Yella Pils. He is holding his iPhone in a purposeful way. Ah. He is recording the conversation already. He will be recording the whole day. Whatever you say *will* be held against you—forever.

That's journalism.

And off we go.

The Sleeve is here today at [Insert Corporate Logo Here] Field: Peyton, Demaryius, C.J., McmAnus, B-Marsh 2, and the Denver defense. I'm going *all in* on nostalgia.

We stand in a slow-moving herd near the stadium's entrance, each person removing keys and phone and walking through a metal detector. What is usually an annoying formality takes on a new significance in light of the terrorists who blew themselves to smithereens outside the stadium in Paris the other day, right before their virgin buddies shot up a concert hall down the street.

When we reach the gate, Mr. Green is turned away because of his bag. He will need to get a locker for his bomb, they say. "Meet you at the seats," he says, and we split up. I walk up the snaked ramp toward the summit, section 511, row 32, seat 7, and stand in line for pig meat as the game starts.

The pigskin flies from Peyton's hand on the Broncos opening series. He is three yards away from the all-time record. The toots are in the limos again. The champagne is on ice again. But it will have to wait until the next series, because Peyton's first throw is a fluttery, buttery ball down the seam to a streaking Vernon Davis, who has a step on his defender. But the football is shot out of the sky, falls short of Vernon, and is intercepted.

Collective groans.

These seats are impressively high up. Just a few rows from the summit. It's a workout to get up here. I'm out of breath as I find my seat, which is occupied by a woman in a leather jacket who assures me that she is in the correct seat. I tell her that she is mistaken, that she is in my seat in section 511. Oh no, she says, this is section 510; section 511 is one section over. No, I say. This is section 511; 510 is one section over. She looks over her shoulder at the big 511 behind us and then graciously relocates with her loquacious lesbian lover.

I sit down and scarf the hot dog. The Chiefs look sharp. The Broncos look blunt. They get the ball back on offense and Peyton completes a four-yard pass to Ronnie Hillman, which breaks the all-time passing yards (ATPY) record.

Yaaaay! screams the crowd out of one side of their mouths. Everyone stands and claps and play stops for a moment to honor one of football's best ambassadors. One of its biggest money-makers; its most illustrious passers; its most beloved; of the royal bloodline; the back on which the NFL's narrative rides. He is the all-time leader. He is still going. He is dragging himself along. He cannot stop.

Peyton presses his lips together and waves to the crowd. He's never been one to milk the accolades. He just wants to play football. He hurries back into the huddle to do what he does best: lead his football team to victory. But just a few plays later, he throws an incompletion on third down and the crowd cannot help themselves. They boo Peyton Manning—the ATPY record holder. They boo him off the field as the punt team comes on.

Mr. Green gets to the seats with two beers. We drink them and talk and Lenny joins us and Peyton throws another interception. Boos rain down on the immortal man. Peyton hobbles off the field with his head down. He looks hurt.

Mr. Green asks many questions and I try to answer them while watching the game. He is echoing conventional journo-wisdom and I find myself getting slightly annoyed when explaining things, but only slightly. I don't want to hurt him.

"What's it like down there? What are they thinking between plays? What's the issue with pain? Are they all just hurting right now?"

"No, there is no pain on a football field. Adrenaline is too high to feel the murmurings of the body. This energy here, you feel it? All of this manic energy is being pumped into their bodies telekinetically. They are possessed. . . . Look there. See that play? That guy just jumped as high as he could in the air and landed on his back, then popped up like nothing happened; a 'routine play,' some would call it. What do you think would happen if you jumped as high as you could and landed on your back right now?"

"I don't know."

"You might die."

"Ha!"

"And the 'routine blocks and tackles': normal stuff, right? Get up and get back into the huddle. Easy. Don't be a pussy, yeah? But what would happen if you walked out of your house in the morning, and on your way to your car, I came at you full speed and hit you as hard as I could, driving you into the ground? Would you get back up and ask for another?"

"If I was making a million dollars a year, yeah!"

"I don't agree. You'd quit after day two. The violence is ceaseless. Your visceral reality would trump any numbers in your bank account."

The Broncos are getting smoked. Peyton throws another interception at the beginning of the second half, then is benched in the fourth quarter for backup Brock Osweiler when the game is all but lost.

The switch elicits cheers from the crowd. Nothing excites Broncos fans more than an unproven quarterback, and Brock is the epitome of this. He has been idling patiently behind Peyton for four years, waiting to unleash the cannon. The Chiefs win handily. The only points scored by the Broncos are in the fourth quarter and Brock is the one who does it. Peyton's body is failing him. Brock is on the rise. The Sleeve is not.

RIP: Bunny Five-Ball Wizard Sleeve: killed by the Broncos.

I'm 3-7.

Fuck.

Buttermilk Old Fashioned

WEEK ELEVEN

KILLING PEYTON

SAN JOSE, CALIFORNIA

Sunny and beautiful back home: it's a perfect day for a round of golf. But today is Coach Zaccheo's funeral. If he didn't have to be here for it, he'd be golfing. He was great at it: probably an 8 handicap. I used to bring him as my ringer for Menlo College best-ball tournaments. I saw him hole-in from 150 yards out and shrug his shoulders like he just made a layup. He was Pioneer's golf coach after retiring from football.

I'm a shitty golfer, stricken with the same athletic propensity as most football players: *attack*. Attack is not a good golf strategy. Coach used to try to help me out on the golf course. Gave me tips, things to think about. Things I tried to think about. Things that helped, until my ego got the better of me again and I swung as if the green were on the moon. He'd just shake his head and laugh. He knew that the same thing that made me good at football made me bad at golf.

Coach Shanahan—an avid golfer—always said that if football players are too good at golf, that's a bad sign. Kickers and quarterbacks are good golfers but the rest of us usually aren't. That explains why Myron was so good. He played quarterback in high school, in college, and was semipro. He understood technique, patience, and posture. When I got to the NFL, I was struck by how similar my new coaches were to Myron: the preparation, the instinct, the strategy, and the ability to lead.

I've had a lot of coaches in my life: soccer, basketball, swimming, football. The best ones don't have anything in common except the ability to convince his team that they will win. That involves a delicate psychology, made unique by the personality of the coach.

Myron was forward-thinking in that way. He downplayed his talents and skills and inflated those of his opponents.

"How's your team looking this year, Coach?"

"Well, we're small, slow, and not very strong."

"How do you feel about the game this week, Coach?"

"We'll be lucky if we can find the field."

Don't give them anything they can use against you. Don't get them riled up. Talk about how good they are. They'll start to believe it. And, conversely, if you convince your own players, by demanding perfection, that they are ready to meet any challenge—no matter how difficult—well, they'll start to believe that, too.

I'm sitting on a bench against the back wall of a church on a hill. The place is overflowing. We had to split up to find seats.

My dad is over there. My mom is on the other side. There's Ryno. There's Wangs. Everyone is here.

A large photo sits on an easel near the pulpit—Myron the Proud Patriarch—smiling at the congregation with that twinkle in his eye. The one that says: *C'mon, you're better than that!* I see it in the eyes of his eleven grandchildren, stronger than they realize, preparing to meet their newest challenge—a life without their hero.

In the climactic moment of my high school football career, in the fourth quarter of our homecoming game against division rival Westmont High School, we found ourselves facing fourth and 10, from their forty-yard line, tied 21–21 with three minutes left in the game. Wangs had thrown it to me down the left sideline on the previous play. I was well covered and couldn't get my hands on it anyway. Incomplete. Coach called a timeout.

Ex-quarterbacks who become coaches have a unique bond with the quarterback of their team. Unique. Volatile. And very mental. The psychology that Coach Zaccheo used on our team as a whole was refined to a laser beam on Wangs, who took it on the chin, every single day.

You're better than that, Justin!

Wangs looked at the first-down marker and unsnapped his chinstrap, then jogged to the sideline. Coach stepped onto the field to meet him, looking through his dark sunglasses and fisherman's hat at the scoreboard in the south end zone.

"What do you think, Coach?"

"Well—what do *you* think, Justin?"

"Let's run the same play," said Wangs without hesitation. "We'll get it."

"Okay, Justin—do it."

Do it. You know better than I do. It's your team now.

Wangs jogged back to the huddle with a look of total confidence. It *was* his team, and now he knew it.

"Hut, *hut*," the ball was snapped, Wangs took five steps and dropped a pearl to me down the left sideline for a thirty-yard gain. We scored on the next play and followed with a defensive goal-line stand as the clock ran out to win the game.

Thanks, Coach. We'll take it from here.

THURSDAY

Bunny Sleeve is circling the drain at 3-7. It might serve us well to start thinking about things a little differently. Taking a cue from some of my old coaches, I've decided to switch up the routine and take the guys bowling. Throw them a bone. They're beat up, they're tired, they've been working hard, and it just hasn't come together. It's not that we're not good enough, it's that we're not clicking. We need to bond as a team, and throwing a weighted ball down a wooden lane at some upright pins is the way to do it. The bowling alley is right down the street. The buses are outside.

"Tracy!"

"Yes, Coach."

"We're going bowling. Do you want to come?"

"I probably shouldn't, Coach. I have a lot of work to do."

"Oh, c'mon, Trace! Everyone could use a little break."

"No, Coach, I should stay."

"Okay, Tracy, I'm sorry, let me rephrase. This is a *team-sanctioned* event, okay? We are losing, Tracy, in case you didn't notice. And if we keep losing, if we don't make the playoffs, then we're all getting pink slips. You got me? I need every swinging dick in this place moving in the same direction if we're going to turn this around. You got me?"

"Yes, Coach."

"So I'll see you on the bus in ten minutes?"

"Yes, Coach."

"Oh, and, uh, Tracy?"

"Yes, Coach?"

"Bring your bowling shoes."

FRIDAY

Tony Romo watches *SportsCenter*. He knows what they've been saying about him. He isn't going to let these assholes write his eulogy. So he's coming back from his broken collarbone a bit earlier than expected. He is the good soldier, brimming with positivity that the 2-7 Cowboys can go on a run and win this whole thing. "We are not dead yet!" he proclaims as the orchestra plays.

Although I don't believe him, this blind optimism is *exactly* what the Sleeve needs to get back on track.

(That and bowling! More on that in a minute.)

So now that Peyton and Andrew Luck are dead and buried in ESPN's 2015 boneyard, the American Football Illuminati (AFI) turns its arrows on some new heroes. This week it's Aaron Rodgers. After Tom Brady, he has been the tallest tree in the Elite Quarterback Forest. But Aaron had a couple of average games the last few weeks and the Packers lost both of them. Now they're blaming his social life. Maybe his girlfriend, Olivia Munn, is distracting him. Don't play into it, Olivia!

Kill the narrative.

Look at Tom Brady! He's chopping up the narrative in itty-bitty pieces and sending unmarked packages to guesthouses in the Adirondacks. The Patriots are undefeated and Brady is playing perhaps his best season after being accused of cheating by the AFI.

Spite is a hell of a drug.

Life works better with a few enemies. Brady sees only haters when he looks around. He sees only doubters. He sees only little experts who call for his head.

He sees the field as a canvas on which to paint, "Fuck the World!"

Bill Belichick and the rest of the organization reap the rewards. Belichick gains the genius moniker de facto. Genius by proxy. Dr. Osmosis.

The Patriot Way is the Brady Way.

But we've got a totally different dilemma over here at Bunny Sleeve. We are failing. I need to kill another of my own narratives. A big one: *the* big one. You know where this is going. I realized it yesterday at the bowling alley. Bowling went really well, by the way. All of the guys had a good time. I really felt like we were able to forget about our four-game losing streak and relax. I'm pretty sure a few of the guys went outside and smoked some weed. Truth is—and I'm going to level with you here—as a coach, I don't mind the weed smokers. I really don't. Shit, we do our homework. We know which guys burn before we ever sign them. High school coaches, college coaches, teachers, friends, family, neighbors, RAs in their dorms, campus cops, ex-girlfriends: we talk to them all. We know what we're getting into. And you want to know something? This is kind of a preliminary finding, but as a staff, we are starting to chart our players and what substances they take to deal with this brutal business. Because—and I'm just gonna shoot it to you straight again here—no one is playing this game without drugs. No one. It's just a fact. It's too painful, too counterintuitive. So the question becomes, what drugs are our guys taking? Pain pills? Weed? Adderall? Alcohol? Molly? Cocaine? Heroin? Have a look at that list of substances. Which one do you think makes the best football players?

You guessed it: good old-fashioned marijuana.

Our highly scientific studies are showing that the weed guys are actually healthier, as a group, than the pain pill guys or the alcohol guys. The hard-drug guys never make it past training camp. But the weed fellas also heal faster than our pain pill guys. And one of the interesting things we've found is that the weed guys are actually *smarter* football players. We chart mental mistakes, errors, penalties, and things like that. We chart *everything*. And what we've found is that our marijuana smokers commit fewer assignment errors and fewer penalties than the pain pill guys. They are also faster to correct mistakes they do make, no matter how complicated our game plans get.

And! Check this out. We're finding that the weed guys suffer brain injuries at a *smaller rate*, and of those who do sustain brain injuries, those who medicate with marijuana afterward recover significantly faster and have a much smaller recidivism rate. So despite the league office's firm stance against the plant as a medicine, we see things a bit differently here at the Sleeve, and don't give our players shit for doing something that helps them on the field. We're trying to win a championship, for Christ's sake!

So the fellas got high and did some bowling. And wouldn't you know it! The stoners bowled better, too. Everyone had a great time.

Well, everyone but Peyton. He looked miserable. Poor guy's falling apart. He couldn't even bowl. He just sat there shifting in his seat, trying to get comfortable. Of course he's been playing like shit. His body is fucked. He can't get anything on his throws because the game has ravaged him. His feet are ruined; ribs, back, neck, hips. Not only that, but he just looks sad. It's been like this all year. His season is likely over, especially with Brock playing well and the Broncos winning.

I know what I have to do now.

"Tracy!"

"Yes, Coach."

"Good times at the bowling alley yesterday, huh?"

"Yes, Coach. It was fun."

"Did I see that right? Did you bowl a 234?"

"I did, Coach."

"Wow! Impressive, Tracy. Really impressive!"

"Thanks, Coach."

"And did I see you stepping outside with a few of our guys before we got started?"

"I don't know, Coach. Did you?"

"I think I did, Tracy. Don't worry, whatever floats your kite."

"Thanks, Coach."

"Okay, well, now for business. Today is the day I hoped would never come, Tracy. Send in Peyton, please."

"Peyton?"

"That's right, Peyton!"

"Are . . . you sure about that?"

"Of course I'm fucking sure, Tracy! Send him in!"

". . . Yes, Coach."

I take a deep breath as Peyton walks into my office. He has a look I wasn't expecting. He appears very relaxed. His face is slackened and his eyes are smiling. He sits down and puts both arms on the armrests.

"Well, Pey—"

"So this is what these chairs feel like!" He leans back. "I always wondered. Hmm! More comfortable than I'd have thought. And you can barely tell it's a trapdoor. Where's the button? Under your desk? It's obvious you put a lot of work into it. That speaks to your integrity, Coach. I've always respected the way you handled things. Thank you for that. You know . . . ever since I was a kid, it's weird . . . *this* is the moment I've been dreaming of. *This moment!* Not the records. Not the touchdowns. Not the Pro Bowls. Not the Super Bowls. But *this* moment *right here.*"

He looks down at the armrests, then up at the ceiling, then

back in my eyes. "The moment some never-was coach tells me that I'm not good enough anymore . . . It used to keep me up at night, Coach. It used to choke me. I couldn't breathe. I couldn't think. All I could do was keep throwing, keep practicing, keep studying, keep moving; otherwise I'd have had a nervous breakdown. It was the only thing that ever mattered to me: the *end* . . . I thought it would break me, Coach. . . . And you know what? I feel fine. I feel great. I feel—I don't know. I feel like someone else. I feel lighter. I swear to you, when Tracy just called me in, something lifted off of me, Coach. All of my aches and pains: they just fucking vanished! Two minutes ago! Gone! It's like I've been living in someone else's body for my whole life, Coach. And now it's time for me to let go. I can say that honestly—I have no fear. Now press it," he said. "I'm ready. Go on, press the button."

Salty tears pour down my face. I try to say something and choke, spitting up a little bit. I wipe my mouth and look at the ground.

"Don't cry, Coach. This is a happy day. Go ahead. Press it."

The tears fall from my chin, darkening the blue carpet. I wipe my cheeks and sniffle, then reach under the desk with my right hand, just like always, and press the button. Nothing. It's jammed! It's never jammed before! I press it again. Nothing again!

"Jesus *Christ*! Tracy! Sorry, Peyton, it's the—"

"C'mon," he says. "Send me home. Let's go, Coach. I'm ready. Press the fucking button!" I keep pressing it but it won't go. Something is stuck. Peyton chuckles and leans forward in his chair, reaches over, and pounds on my desk with his large hand—once, twice, three times. On the third time, we both hear it fall back into place. Peyton straightens in his chair. "All right now, Coach. Don't make me wait any longer . . . Send me home."

Click!

The bottom drops out and Peyton falls through to the killing floor. I hear the dogs descend on him. *Shit!* I usually don't look down and watch. I don't want to see the blood. But I can't help myself this time. Something in me needs to see this. I stand up and peer over my desk and into the darkness. Peyton sits on the dirt, illuminated by some green light, with the pack of dogs on top of him, tails wagging, licking his face.

"Tracy!"

"Yes, Coach."

"Get me Brock Osweiler!"

"Yes, Coach."

"And, Tracy?"

"Yes, Coach?"

"Bring me some Kleenex."

MONDAY

Sometimes all you need is to switch up the routine. The Sleeve got a much-needed win yesterday. We are still a long shot to make the playoffs—but a long shot is better than no shot at all. We are 4-7. The Broncos beat the Bears yesterday in Chicago with Brock Osweiler at the helm to get to 8-2. It was an action-packed game for Bunny Sleeve as much of my lineup was on the field: Demaryius Thomas, Alshon Jeffrey, Martellus Bennett, the whole Broncos defense. Triple nostalgia! Still, I found myself dozing off on my couch and gorging myself on donuts; three of them, in fact, from the same gentrodonut spot here in Venice.

Three donuts for $12.50!

I nearly swallowed my arugula-lemon toothpick when they gave me the total. After placing the order I stood to the side in a cluster of other customers as we watched an assembly line of well-manicured donut-mongers swaddle each one in lacy tissue paper and lay them down on a bed of rose petals. They were able to gather my three donuts after about ten minutes, placing them in a large box, fit for a dozen.

"Do you have a smaller box? Something I can fit in my backpack."

"But, but, but . . . you might *ruin* them!"

"I'm just going to eat them."

"You're going to do *what*?"

Word came out of San Francisco this week that Kappy is going on injured reserve. He is having surgery on a torn labrum in his nonthrowing shoulder. His season is over. So are his days as a 49er, in all likelihood. His football career, though? Far from done. He will go somewhere new, somewhere he can have a fresh start. Somewhere people respect his talent and his hard work. Somewhere that hasn't been infected by cyber-germs and corporate stadium deals. Somewhere the gentro-hipsters aren't moving in. Somewhere that people still have sex, still go outside.

Enjoy Russia, Kappy! We hardly knew ya.

Tonight I am going to the L.A. premiere of *Concussion*. I pick up my date in West Hollywood and we head to Westwood. She is a singer, actor, producer, writer, and philanthropist named Trudy. She knows this town. She's been in this industry her entire adult life. We park a few blocks away and walk toward the theater. There is a chill in the air. Trudy's heels skip on the pavement as I tell her the whole story of Hollydouche and *Concussion*, expecting her to be surprised. She just laughs and shakes her head.

"Welcome to Hollywood," she says.

"Really? That's normal?"

"Unfortunately, yes."

We turn the corner and see crowds of onlookers cordoned behind metal gates that line the red carpet. Their iPhones are trained to capture the moment, to be squinted at later in solitude.

Will-call chick across the street hands me an envelope with two tickets to the show and two tickets to the after party at the W hotel down the street. I sigh and hand Trudy her ticket and we show it to the security guy who lets us into the Fox Theater.

As we walk into the lobby, I see my friend Scott Fujita, former linebacker for the Saints and Chiefs, accompanied for the evening by his mother, who is beaming. Scott is an eleven-year veteran, three years retired. I met Scott during the East-West Shrine Game in 2002. He played for Cal, me for Menlo. The game was in San Francisco. We struck up a friendship that carried through our time in the league. Saw him twice a year when we played the Chiefs. Saw him at off-season functions. Scott was a longtime NFLPA union rep, well respected in NFL circles; smart, charismatic, connected.

We were both working with Guy in the lead-up to *Concussion*, assuming that we had similar consulting roles. But when Guy stopped returning my calls and filming commenced in Pittsburgh, I texted Scott: "Hey, man, I haven't heard from Peter; are you still involved in the film?"

"Yeah," he responded. "I'm here in Pittsburgh. Filming started yesterday."

Boom. Now I understand. Just over a year later, and here we are standing in the lobby of the Fox Theater. Scott supplied the wisdom, rhetoric, locations, and rationale for the majority of the football scenes, which came out good.

Me? I was at home smoking weed and punching the wooden support beam in my apartment until my knuckles bled. Good lessons, these.

We stand in the lobby laughing about all of it, looking around at our strange new world. Before taking our seats, I grab a bag of popcorn and a bottle of water, all of them lined up on the counter and free. As I put a few pieces into my mouth, I run into an old teammate, Terrell Owens, grabbing popcorn, too.

"Hey, man!"

"Hey, how are you?"

"Good, you?"

"Good, good—what have you been up to?"

"I wrote a book. You're in it!"

"A book? What's it called?"

"Slow Getting Up."

"Cool, I'll check it out."

Once we're seated and the lights go down, Hollydouche is introduced. He takes the microphone and reads from a piece of paper. He says that the movie he thought he was going to make is not the one he made. That it never is. That it takes on a life of its own. And this film, he says, is not about taking down the NFL, or destroying the game of football. It's about a man— an outsider—who fought for what he knew to be true, who exemplified what it meant to be an American, who blah blah blah; echo chamber stuff, mostly.

But here is his main point: This film is not about the men whose brains were discovered to be rotten. It's about a *doctor* and an *actor*, both with impeccable CT scans, who had the courage to follow their convictions. One of them, scientific; one of them, artistic. Both of them, narcissistic.

But who am I kidding? Why am I here? I too am seeking credit. I am the warrior. I deserve the Oscar.

Guy hands the microphone to Will Smith. Will has the glow

of a Real American Movie Star. He owns his personality in a way that is comforting. He is here for us, it says. Will says a few words of thanks, then something like: "Okay, now I'm going to go sit *next* to Dr. Om*alu* and watch my*self* on-*screen*, playing *him*. Sooooo . . ."

The crowd laughs as if hypnotized, then the film starts, and in the company of these strangers it looks different.

Concussion: Now we know what is really at stake when we play football—that which makes us *human*. Our *brains*. Our *lives*. So what is it about this game that makes these men willing to die to make a play? Because the truth is this: every game I was ever in, I was willing to *die* to make the play.

Who doesn't want to watch that?

After the credits, we go to the W and drink free whiskey and eat free crab cakes and brownies and have a nice time. Will Smith's family is there with him, and I observe from a distance the magnetic power of movie stardom, as a cluster of manic people hold iPhones in the air, odd sounds and stomping feet, and two tall model types with bubble butts fawning over Will's son, Jaydon.

Trudy and I and Scott and Brendan Ayanbadejo—another former player—and his wife, plus Matt Willig, stand near the food table talking about the film. There is no test for CTE in living people. There is no way to know if we have it, despite the likelihood that we all do. Them's the odds. Our brains have probably been altered by the game. But some former players are symptomatic and some are not. So what causes the effect? Why are some ravaged, some not? That's the mystery. That's the billion-dollar question. I've had this conversation with several former players: if there was a test, would you want to know?

Do you want to know if you have CTE?

Both Scott and I agree that we do not want to know; otherwise it becomes a self-fulfilling prophecy and we attribute every life hiccup to our degenerative brain disease that will only get worse and worse, the doctors tell us. The snowball rolls downhill. Everyone gets buried.

"I couldn't watch a game for *ten* years," says Matt. "I just started being able to again."

"Have you talked to Peter?" Scott asks me.

"No, I haven't."

"You should go talk to him. He's over there."

"No, I'm good."

"No, I want to see it! Ha!"

"I don't."

Nothing personal—now I get it. Promise the world to everyone and hope for the best. Cast the widest net imaginable, knowing that it doesn't matter if you catch a single fish, because you don't eat seafood.

On the way out, Scott introduces me to Dr. Bennett Omalu. He is a small, smiling man in a dark suit, enjoying the strange trip into the twisted heart of American manhood.

"How many years did you play?" he asks.

"Six."

"And what position?"

"Tight end."

I see him working a quick calculation in his mind.

"Hmmm." He nods and we walk out into the night.

WEEK TWELVE

THE WISHBONE

LOS GATOS, CALIFORNIA

The holiday spirit moves. Tomorrow is Thanksgiving and today I acquired Shaun Draughn on the waiver wire. He is a running back for the struggling Niners and will be taking the bulk of the carries until Carlos Hyde returns from an injury. Kappy's replacement, Blaine Gabbert, threw Draughn the ball eleven times last week. Eleven is a lot of targets. Bunny knows it's all about *targets*. Yahoo charts all of it. But you don't get the ball thrown to you unless the coach dials it up. The organism! The Niners are a diseased organism, lopsided and insecure. No downfield passing game means lots of throws to the running back. You can win by betting on their heavy side. Numbers, man.

So I hit the waiver wire and got Draughn on the Sleeve to bolster my ailing running back group. Of course, I had to cut a guy to do it, and I chose Karlos Williams. Turns out LeSean McCoy is quite healthy, sadly, and taking the majority of the snaps. Karlos took it well. Didn't even blink or cringe or anything when he fell through.

Either way, I need a miracle if I'm going to make the playoffs. I need to win the next two games and I need a few of my friends to lose. It's not an awesome scenario.

THURSDAY

Thanksgivings are for hangovers.

This morning I woke up and took an Uber to Los Gatos, where I left my car last night after chasing the *sweaty moment* in a packed bar. The night before Thanksgiving is always a good party. Everyone is home. Everyone is horny.

On my way home, I stopped by Wangs's place and watched the Lions whoop the Eagles in the first of three Thanksgiving Day NFL games. Football is America's game, that's for sure: it's our noisiest national sacrament. Football adorns Holy Days with meaning, equates the physical sacrifice with the nationalist sentiment. We are good Americans. We play along. We buy the things. We watch the stuff. We eat the beef. But we want more. We need more. We are trying to find ways to get more. To have more. To feel more.

Thanksgiving action!

Wangs is particularly fired up about the point spread in the game between the undefeated Carolina Panthers and the 3-7 Dallas Cowboys. It didn't make any sense! The line was even. It was a pick-'em game. That means that no one was favored.

The Panthers have proven themselves to be a far superior team this season, but the oddsmakers were not convinced. Myth! The Romo Myth moved the line from where it should have been. The myth was of his resurrection and inevitable path to a storybook NFL comeback. "We're going to make a run and win this thing!" he said, and everyone got on board because they want something to believe in. Romo then had to put his body where his mouth was. His broken clavicle was healed enough, he thought, to put the hopes and dreams of America's Team on his back.

And even the professional oddsmakers bought in.

Kill the narrative.

Tony Romo took the field today and threw three interceptions in quick succession; two of them were returned for touchdowns. The Panthers went up 20–3 early on the heels of the dying myth. Then Romo's inevitable resurrection hit a snag called *nature.* In a play not unlike the one that snapped him two months ago, Romo twisted in a way he often does while being tackled and was fallen upon by the defender. The weight of the world was, once again, too much for his skeleton. His collarbone snapped like the twig it isn't.

The disappointment bled through the screen; no one was more disappointed than Tony Romo, who will now blame himself and wonder what he did wrong. Second place on the disappointment scale will be the Dallas Cowboys and Jerry Jones, hoping for some good press and now assuredly getting none.

Coming in a close third place are the millions of fantasy owners who threw their turkey legs at the television when he went down and did not get up. Count Rocky among them. Rocky bought into the Romo hype and started him. Thanksgiving action! But Romo scored him −9.76 points with that performance. (He will go on to lose to Skone: 208.06–205.34.) What will be another long nightmarish climb back up to national relevance for Tony Romo becomes just another trip to the waiver wire for the fickle fantasy crowd.

Fourteen million trapdoors.

Two hundred million dogs.

Carolina won handily, 44–13, led by Cam Newton, wunderkind. The 11-0 Carolina Panthers are using a model that the AFI says they can't win with. Cam Newton, Carolina's quarterback, plays the position as a new-age quarterback. Cam is an evolved athlete. Cam Newton is the model of the mold breaker. Cam is the NFL's MVP thus far. He runs the ball when the ball must be run. He throws when it must be thrown. He can do what must be done because no restrictions have been put on him. Do what you have to do to make the play. Since Cam's physical abilities allow it, he can make any play on the field. To gain control of your own power in the NFL is difficult. Your name must be so big, your body of work so dynamic, that public opinion of the team depends on your performance; then a coach will relent and hand the reins to a proven golden ticket.

It certainly helps that Cam's coach is Ron Rivera, a former NFL player, who is not intimidated by Cam's personality. This allows Cam to be himself on and off the field, which is the catalyst to his renaissance.

Food! My sister Carol cooked a delicious feast, despite her oven breaking at a most inopportune time, forcing a meat-heating innovation. Brother-in-law Jeff barbecued the bird in a pan and it cooked wondrously, though it delayed the start of dinner by forty-five minutes, a time happily spent watching the last of the three games—Chicago versus Green Bay—with my family on the couch.

THE WISHBONE | 159

I did not start Jay Cutler this week for Bunny Sleeve. I'm
going with Brock Osweiler against the Patriots, and so I watched
Jay play with some mixed emotions. I hoped the Bears won,
which they did, but I also hoped that Jay's numbers were average enough so that I did not regret benching him. This ended
up being the case. The Bears won in Green Bay on the night
that Bret Favre and Bart Starr were honored as forever gods in
Packerland.

Meanwhile, Aaron Rodgers struggled in the rain and armed
the naysayers with new ammunition to shoot at him over the
next week and a half. As the game ended on an incomplete
fourth-down pass to the end zone, I heard a high-pitched scream
from some luxury suite.

I think it was Olivia Munn.

The extra time before dinner gave me the chance to chat
with Tal, my niece's Israeli boyfriend. "This is *football*?" he said
sarcastically, not yet knowing he was sitting next to a former
NFL meathead. Not anymore, Tal. Turkey meat. Let's eat.

That night, belly full and mind adrift, I dream that I sneak
into the Broncos facility, aided by a few of the equipment
guys. I'm trying to stay undetected, milling around the indoor
field and taking photos of some questionable artwork: a Tech-
nicolor drawing of Bill Cosby with a caption that reads: "Don't
say I didn't warn you!"

What? Soon, the room starts filling with players and coaches,
and I slip outside, where many fans are waiting. Everyone comes
out here and gathers around Coach Kubiak. I find myself near
the front, a few feet from Koob, and I panic. I have to get out
of here. I don't want to be seen. I pull my hat low and shimmy
through the crowd, escaping out the back. Only now I can't find
my car. It's not where I left it! Up and down the steps I go, into

the parking garage, through row after row of tan and gray cars and trucks: it's nowhere. It was *right here!* As I ascend another set of parking garage stairs, I awake to the sound of my niece running through the hall. The day has begun, like it or not.

SUNDAY

Tales from the *Sunday Glut*: today, Bunny Wizard Sleeve Five-Ball's fantasy football season will either survive for another week, or be killed outright. The holiday was treacherous on my innards. Yesterday I left San Jose and drove back to L.A. to deal with the aftermath alone. Thanksgiving-induced constipation (TIC) and I'm all out of Movantik.

In my brand-new onesie of marbleizing fat cells, I sit on the couch and watch Sunday football. Despite my sunny outlook in the face of inevitable demise, it's clear very early on today that it is not to be for the Sleeve. Our last-place team, Participation Trophy, is having his best performance of the year all over my face.

Twomp's number one overall pick, Adrian Peterson, is running crazy: 45.70 points. Sammy fucking Watkins scores 40.80. I wonder if Twomp is paying attention. If he is, I know that he is laughing at me in his high-pitched cackle. But I don't know what he is doing. I know what I'm doing! Sitting on my couch. I decide to get high. Higher. Highest. Then I get thirsty. Thirstier. Thirstiest! I open the refrigerator and a tumbleweed blows across the main shelf. Hand to mouth—bare-bones—that's how I like to live these days. I write better with empty cupboards. Also, having no food or drink in my apartment guarantees that I'll eventually leave to find sustenance.

So despite my crippling fears, I step outside of my apartment and into the world, to get some coffee. I *need* this cup of coffee.

I mean—it's worth the risk of human contact. I turn into the lounge and sitting on the couch biting her lip with a journal in her lap is my friend Allison.

Wake up, Nate! Words now. The cellophane breaks on my bubble and I'm of the world, like it or not. Now you are an Adult American Man and you must act like one. Have a conversation. Nod and say yes, yes, oh definitely yes! Pay attention to her words. She is saying them, after all. Give her the respect her heart deserves.

She says she wants to move to a farm, a ranch, and get away from L.A.; get away from all of these . . . *people*, driving up the rent and driving out the moment. Now Venice is Silicon Beach and Portland is Silicon Forest. The gap between the rich and the poor is growing. More tech nerds able to pay $5,000 for a two-bedroom apartment equals more homeless people milling around outside. Be careful what you fish for. Predators flock to easy prey. Remember the lion!

"Where do you want to get a ranch? Back home?" She's from the South.

"No, not back home. It's, too, I don't know, too much family back there."

"Yeah, I hear you. Then you get pulled back into everyone's drama, right?"

"Yeah, how did you know? Did I tell you that?"

"No, I think that happens to everyone. Where do you want your farm?"

"I don't know . . . maybe Santa Barbara?"

"Ha! It's going to be a very small farm! Maybe like the size of this room. Chickens in that corner, horses in that one."

"Oh, whatever! You don't have to kill my dream like that!"

This is a problem of mine. I have an itch to kill the fairy tale, if you couldn't already tell.

I say goodbye to Allison and reenter my Sunday football bubble, never again to exit! That was terrifying, interacting with another human like that.

I take another bong rip and settle in for an extended Bunny Five-Ball funeral. Going into the night game between the 10-0 Patriots and the 8-2 Broncos, it will take a completely dominant performance by the Broncos in snow and freezing temperatures for me to beat Twomp. He is out to a sizable lead. He also has Tom Brady and the Patriots defense going tonight. This is it for me.

But for the Denver Broncos, the team of actual men who play actual football against the actual Patriots, it will simply take scoring more points than their opponents to win.

Snow covers [Insert Corporate Logo Here] Field, lines are shoveled off during TV timeouts; white crowns collect on players' helmets, breath comes out of face masks like cold smoke, crystalized confetti scrapes the high-def screen, and I sit inside my bubble of Sunday glut, with TIC and coffee and a newspaper that will not be read.

Go Brock! Go! Brock Osweiler stands tall in the snow, throws the ball to the guys with hands, and lets them run. Let them run!

Peyton stands stage right, dressed in sweats. Peyton knows. Peyton knows everything. We've all left him for dead. The camera pans past him and we make eye contact. I know that what I have done to him is wrong. I know that I have angered the gods. But what choice did I have?

The Broncos beat the Patriots in overtime on a 48-yard touchdown run by C. J. Anderson, my first pick of the draft three months ago. C.J.! He could have helped Bunny Sleeve today. We didn't get much out of anyone this week. Anyone except B-Marsh, that is. My heart! I know we're swirling down the toilet right now, but these small victories keep me afloat, and watching B-Marsh score 42.10 points was one of those moments. But it dissipated quickly, and now it's just the darkness setting in. The grim realization of inevitable defeat. Truth is, C.J. had a great game, but he wouldn't have won it for the Sleeve. And that's the reason why he was on my bench today. He hasn't been scoring a lot of *fantasy* points this year. He didn't pan out for *me*. Same goes for lots of other fantasy owners, whose lives have been turned upside down by the wasted draft pick. C.J. has been subjected to cyberattacks by button pushers who call him worthless on Twitter and Instahate. Ronnie Hillman has been taking the bulk of the snaps for the Broncos, so I benched C.J.

But Broncos coach Gary Kubiak did not bench C.J. He fed him the rock in the Mile High Snow Globe, and C.J. proved his worth to the sky, fantasy gods be damned.

MONDAY

Tonight the Ravens played the Browns in what many call a "meaningless game." Players on winning teams become worthy of praise; players on losing teams become worthy of ridicule. But there are always equal numbers of each: wins and losses, winners and losers. No matter. Run the losers out of town. They blow! Let's get some new losers in here!

Here's an analogy:
There is a rectangle made up of thirty-two identical squares. Each square is two inches deep. I'm holding *one pound of sand*. It represents a finite number of wins and losses. In every contest, there must be a winner and there must be a loser—or, in very rare cases, a tire.

I pour the sand into the rectangle, filling the squares, some more than others. I cover the rectangle with a glass top and shake it up once a week. Sand moves around from square to square. More sand over here; less sand over here. But always sand: always *one pound of sand.*

When I'm finally done shaking sand around in early February, one square will have the most grains, and will be called a champion. Is this square bigger than the others? Better? Or is it just a square with more sand?

Keep the game on mute and you'll have one answer.

Turn it up and you'll have another.

WEEK THIRTEEN

JUST DESSERT

This is how the Bunny dies. It's the last week of my fantasy season. I'm out of the playoffs. It's a strange feeling, coming into work like this, knowing that I've failed. Knowing that all of the sleepless nights, all of the film watching, all of the practices, all of the hours spent sitting on the toilet trying desperately to squeeze out just one solitary petrified turd: it was all for nothing. I am a failure and I know it. I walk into my office and am surprised that there is no pink slip on my desk. It's coming any day now, that's for sure.

I open my drawer and look at the pistol. Yeah, it's loaded. So what? I keep it there to remind myself of the easy way out, what a coward would do when the going got tough. Not me. Not now. But I will say, gosh—how great it would be to float away once and for all, to unclench what has been clenched, to wear some normal clothes, to sleep past 4 a.m., to take a healthy shit; to live, to laugh, to love!

Love? Do you remember me? I remember thee!

"Tracy?"

"Yes, Coach?"

"Can you come in here, please?"

"Yes, Coach."

Tracy walks into my office wearing a white sweater and some kind of tan pants and boot combination. She is beautiful. This is true. But she's so much more, and I have never figured out how to tell her. How to let down my guard and be someone that she can trust. Where do I even start? Hell, she is ten times smarter than I am. She doesn't belong here. She got a sports marketing degree from UCLA and here she is as my fucking *secretary*. And she's never complained. Not once. She never slacks off. She's always on time. She's single, too, I think. But I don't know, because I don't ask, because I don't know what to say to her. I don't know how to talk to her about . . . life, ya know? *Life!* Is *this* life? Sitting in this swivel chair, mesh shorts riding up my ass crack, smelling my armpits, watching film, calling coaches, having meetings, patting guys on the back, chewing Copenhagen and sunflower seeds?

Is this all I am?

"Tracy, have a seat." She sits down with her knees touching. What miracles unleash when they part? "So, I'm just going to give it to you straight, Trace. I really don't know what's going to happen to us after this week. You'd think that with back-to-back championships the last two years, we'd be safe . . . but I'm not sure. Everyone's so fickle now, Tracy. It's championship or bust. They don't understand that it's hard to win it all. Shit! It's nearly damned impossible! They don't understand that *everyone* is good at this level, that there ain't no losers! *Sheeeit!* Listen to me! Sounds like a loser talking, huh?"

"No, Coach! That is *not* true! *You* are *not* a loser." Tracy sits forward in her seat and looks at me dead straight. "You are a *winner* and you need to be proud of what you've done here. These people . . . these *fans* . . . or whatever they call themselves . . . do you really think they'll ever be satisfied? Don't you re*member* the last two years? Did it *feel* like we won the championship?"

"No."

"That's right . . . it didn't. It felt like we lost, Coach. You were more stressed than you were the year before. The success only brought more scrutiny. More expectations. More eyeballs on you, Coach. I've watched it happen. I've seen you change— physically, emotionally. You even smell different, Coach. Ever since I was a little girl, I wanted to be a part of a football team . . . part of this." She points around the room to the framed photos on the wall. "Sure, my dad was a coach, but that's not why I wanted to be here. Not because of my *dad*. I wanted to be here because *I* believed in the *game*. Note, I said *believed*, Coach. Because you know what? . . . I don't believe anymore. Not in *this*." She motions to the papers all over my desk. "Look at you! What the hell are these?" She picks up a stack of them. "Who is com- piling these? You? Jesus, Coach! You used to say that only losers check the stats. Winners *chuck* the stats. Remember? Well, look at you now, Coach! I guess you're right. By your own definition, you *have* become a loser. You have become what you always de- spised. Now you're no different from the little men on TV who sneer and laugh and call out *our* men for not being *man enough*. And what do you do about it, Coach? How do you fight them? You cut *Peyton*! *Ha!* In the *middle* of the season! Your season was over anyway and you didn't have the decency to let him finish it off on the team he inspired to greatness in the first place. All of the guys down in the locker room fell in love with the game looking up to men like Peyton, men you had the honor of drafting and coaching. But you couldn't even let him go out in peace, could you? You couldn't keep him around and let him grieve with his brothers. You threw him to the dogs, Coach, like everyone else out there. You're just like them, after all . . . and I can't stand behind this anymore."

She leans back and takes a deep breath and looks around the room.

"This morning when I was getting ready, I cried, Coach. I cried because I knew that this was over for me—all of it. I cried because of what I knew I had to do. And I cried for you, Coach. I cried for *you*. Every single day when I came in here to work, to do my job, I thought that *maybe* today is the day that Coach will ask me something *real*. Maybe today is the day that Coach doesn't stare at my tits or ask me to pick something up just so he can look at my ass. Maybe today is the day that Coach won't make a comment to one of his players about my body. Maybe today is the day that Coach will be a real man. Maybe today is the day that I'll *actually* get to meet my boss, as a human being. . . . But that day never came, Coach. It never came. And eventually I stopped expecting it. And now . . . well, now I understand it, and it took meeting someone *else* to make me realize it. Someone who doesn't wear mesh shorts to work every day. And you know what? I'm finally—

Click.

I don't have time for this shit. If we don't win this game and finish on a high note, we're all going to the dogs: me, Peyton, Tracy, everybody. You don't quit on a play and you don't quit on your team! You finish! You always finish.

Every day.

No matter what.

WEDNESDAY

I drive to Irvine to visit with my old agent, Ryan Tollner, and his cousin Bruce. Together they started Rep1 Sports and now represent forty-seven active NFLers: some superstars, most not.

Their offices are spacious. Behind the modern front desk is a young secretary holding a telephone. Behind her is a large conference room and collection of four or five offices with glass walls around a common area that has cushy couches and round tables with chairs and flat-screen TVs and a Ping-Pong table and shuffleboard and framed jerseys and Fatheads and photos on the wall.

Ryan isn't here yet so I sit at the round table with Bruce and another agent, Chase, and talk about *this* book. I try to explain some of the angles I'm working on and it sounds stupid coming out of my mouth. Talking about a book in progress is a bad idea. It only makes me second-guess myself. I tell them about the trapdoor. And about Tracy. And I'm surprised that they don't jump up and do a back handspring right there and pre-order a hundred copies. It's a lesson that must be constantly learned as a writer.

No one gives a fuck.

I ask Chase if the players are monetizing their fantasy football value. He says not really. The deals that DraftKings and FanDuel have with certain NFL teams and with the NFLPA are not getting to the players. That revenue isn't added to the league's "total revenue" figure, which determines player salary. It's a team-licensing fee, similar to paying for the use of a team's logo. The individual is simply an extension of that team logo; the assumption is that he has no value without that logo, that the team itself is the value and the moneymaker.

As for the NFLPA, the money they get from DraftKings also doesn't seem to reach the players. Apparently there are 130

NFLPA employees with salaries exceeding 125K, and while league revenue has skyrocketed and union dues have increased, royalty payments for the players have gone down.

The NFLPA has a somewhat contentious relationship with the eight hundred licensed agents. "Licensed" means that they pay yearly licensing fees to the NFLPA, which is threatening to reduce their maximum allowable percentage from 3 percent down to 2 percent of a player's contract. Three percent is already the lowest of the major professional sports. And since NFL contracts are not guaranteed, it makes it difficult for agents to carve out a living in the field. And with eight hundred of them, the competition is stiff for the crop of 250 or so college prospects who come out each year.

It might be too late.

For everyone.

Ryan and Bruce represent Ben Roethlisberger, quarterback of the Pittsburgh Steelers, who was pulled out of the game on Sunday after "self-reporting" some blurriness in his peripheral vision. He was then placed in the league's "concussion protocol," which ended his game. The blurry vision lasted less than an hour, and he reported no more symptoms, but the "self-reporting" made headlines and was championed as a significant stride in the concussion dilemma. Media outlets picked up the story, celebrating coach Mike Tomlin's role in keeping Ben off the field for the good of his brain.

This was the feel-good concussion story the league needed after last week, in which Rams quarterback Case Keenum was pulled down from behind on a tackle that made his head bounce off the artificial turf like a medicine ball. He grabbed his helmet and rolled around, woozy, unaware, then was pulled to his feet by a teammate and stayed in the game. Forty seconds is plenty of time to pull it together.

Boxers only have ten.

There are supposedly independent neurologists who are watching games now, with their fingers on a button up in a booth, ready to alert someone that a player has suffered a brain injury and something must be done to get them off the field. They're still working out the kinks.

The kicker here with the situation in Pittsburgh is that Big Ben doesn't think he has a concussion. He thinks he is fine. As do all of the other football players who have been banging heads their whole lives and are familiar with what it feels like to get their bells rung. A nerd in a luxury box will not know when *I'm* hurting. That's for sure. And what do you think my coach will say to me when I come off the field and tell him that the last hit I took really *hurt*, Coach—I mean, I feel a little dizzy and, like, ya know?

He may hand me a trash bag right there.

"Go clean out your locker!"

Each time a player sees the "concussion protocol" applied, it cements his need to circumvent it.

ESPN feels the heat of complicity. During a stoppage of time during Monday night's game, they described the league's concussion protocol:

1. When a potential concussion is identified, the player shall be *removed immediately from the field.*
2. The NFL team physician and the unaffiliated neurotrauma consultant (UNC) will:
    a. Review the video of the play
    b. Perform a focused neurological exam
3. Madden Rule: If there is a suspicion of a concussion, the player will be escorted to the locker room where the team physician and UNC will perform a full assessment.
4. If the player is diagnosed with a concussion, there is NO same day return to play.

5. If the player passes the exam, he will be monitored for symptoms throughout the game.

Sounds like a real drag.

Ryan and I go to lunch and on the way out run into former quarterback Trent Edwards, one of his clients. He is working with a virtual reality company on a product that allows a player to put on a set of VR goggles and see the entire field from a quarterback's perspective. Look left, look right, look behind you: you see the whole field and everyone on it. This is a tool intended to give mental reps to quarterbacks. It lets him see plays develop, coverages, blitzes, alignments, etc., more effectively seeing the field and making his reads. In essence, it turns football preparation into a video game, injecting more delicate fingers into the equation, filling the athlete's head with more jargon, more expectations, more judgment, more bullshit. I'm not a fan. The less I hear from you—you soft-bellied watcher—the better I will play and the more I will enjoy it.

At lunch in the cafeteria they share with Asics corporate headquarters, I tell Ryan about cannabidiols and brain trauma. He finds it interesting but knows very little about the world of NFL pain management. He tells me—and I realize as much as he is saying it—that his players don't tell him what they take. Makes plenty of sense. I kept mine to myself, too. Although Ryan was my friend, he was still aligned with the NFL machine that had the power to end me. This means that players truly have no outlet for an honest expression or discussion about pain and pain management. It is forge ahead until I'm dead, keep my pain to myself, and keep the weed to myself, too.

Never tell anyone anything ever.

On my way home, driving up the 405, I hear a report on the radio of another active shooter, this one just down the road in San Bernardino. (Where I'm from, an active shooter was someone who jacked off a lot.) A husband and wife sprayed a room of coworkers with bullets, then sped off and shot it out with the cops four hours later. They both died in the exchange, and now there's another media frenzy.

This new fight against radical dipshits will take cooperation and creativity from the media. Do not deify them. Humiliate them. Do not espouse their ideologies. Espouse the contradictions. Espouse their foolishness. Laugh at their cowardice. I don't know. What am I going to do? Lock myself in a bunker and tweet about it?

> Carry on, says the sun
> Reflecting off the California coastline
> Behold the blue glass landslide
> Ashore of the only opposite

SATURDAY

The holiday spirit moves me.

My Saturday morning bike ride to Self Espresso is stifled by the zigzagging route of a Christmas-themed 5K run through the blocked-off streets of Venice. Local ambitionists wearing all red and Santa hats—bells jingling and lips parched—skip and gallop along the asphalt.

I roll by them on the sidewalk, going in the opposite direction. These runners come in all shapes and ages. Some look to be in agony, some in total bliss. Some are talking to each other; others are listening to music. What they all have in common is that they're participating in something that I cannot. My body will not allow jogging on concrete.

A six-foot-six, 260-pound fifty-year-old man with a knee brace and a red spandex shirt shuffles past me, inches from death. He's a superior athlete to me; it's obvious. Ah, there goes a child, sprinting through the street, total freedom on his face! Stupid fucking kid. He has no idea. Fuck these people, I'm getting a donut.

"Will you be enjoying the donut now or will you be enjoying the donut later?" asks the donut swaddler.

"What the fuck did you just ask me?"

She clicks the plastic container closed and hands it to me and I backpack it.

Watching those runners this morning reminds me that I need to work on my ankle. I've been neglecting it. No one is telling me what to do. I will then do nothing. My insurance is not as inclusive as it was when I played in the NFL. I got five years of postcareer health insurance—now I'm on my own. My five years was up last year, then I transferred it over to COBRA.

But the COBRA plan is different. I don't know why or how, of course, because I only speak football. But now I'm coming out of pocket for significant percentages of physical therapy sessions. I need hands on my ankle to mobilize the joint. I need some help. I need a professional. My COBRA runs out very soon and I will have to purchase a new insurance plan altogether, just in time for my body to fall apart completely!

Back in 2011, I filed a worker's compensation lawsuit in California, and by 2012 it was almost done. Doctors, MRIs, X-rays, depositions: it was all over except the judgment. But then the NFL owners pushed a bill through the state senate—AB 1309—that prevented players from filing their suit in California, and it shelved thousands of pending cases—many in much worse shape than me. My lawyer kept kicking the can down the road, saying that if I provide this document or that document, then they might reopen my case, because I'm a California native and resident. So I dug through old bills and pay stubs, mildewed from the flood, and scanned them all, hoping it would provide a solid enough connection to California for them to see my case.

But nothing came of it. I'm a number to them. I have no lobby-ists. No recourse. That ship has sailed. They'll make sure I don't get paid. They'll make sure none of us do.

So I deal with it. I'm tough. I'm a warrior. But I need medi-cine, for lots of things. The list of physical and neurological ail-ments I have would be treated in Western medicine by multiple pharmaceuticals. That's something my insurance will definitely pay for: pills! Buckets of pills are a phone call away. The indus-try is ready to kill my pain for me, ready to clear a nice spot on the riverbank for me and give me a bell to ring when I need my meds. Then they'll hand me the remote control, so I can sit there and watch it all wash away. But I don't want your pills.

I want my mind!

I wonder what it would take for an insurance company to cover cannabis for its patients. I know for certain that Cigna saves money on me because I don't take any pills. But is that good for their business? Likely not. Their premiums go up when I need pills. They pay the pharmaceutical companies; we pay them. What happens when the pill orders go down? Revenue for Merck and Pfizer goes down. Insurance premiums go down. Insurance companies' revenues go down. Movantik sales go down.

But scientists are discovering things about cannabis that warrant our consideration. For one, according to several new reports and studies, it's an effective PTSD medication. Twenty-two U.S. veterans commit suicide every day in this country. Films like *Concussion* highlight the suicidal tendencies of the former football player, but the real scourge is happening with our soldiers: twenty-two every day. Americans. Warriors. Gone, at their own hand: the same hand that steadied its rifle and squeezed the trigger on foreign soil to protect your delicate fingers. It turns out that cannabis can help them, too. And science is explaining why.

Cannabis suppresses dream recall. When I smoke it at night, I fall asleep fast, and when I wake up in the morning, I have no memory of whatever happened in my head. For those who are tormented by nightmares or insomnia, it allows them to sleep. When I do not use cannabis, it takes me longer to fall asleep, and when I do sleep, my dreams are confusing and sometimes violent.

When I dream of football something always goes wrong. I can't find the stadium or my cleats are missing or the locker room door is locked and the coach is calling my name. Sometimes I wake up with cuts on my fingers. Seriously. I wonder if when we fall asleep in this world, do we wake up in another one? Trick question: of course we do. I just want to find out who is biting my fingers on the other side. But I can't remember! Because I have PTSD! And I smoke too much pot!

So anyway, it's week 13, the last game of the year for old Bunny Sleeve. Peyton is gone. Tracy is gone. But surprisingly, a lot of my core guys are still around. So I'm loading up my starting lineup with all of the nostalgia I can muster. It is my send-off for the men who gave me their all this year. Typically, season-long fantasy rosters are decimated by injury and therefore change significantly throughout the season. But my guys are still around.

Still fighting.

Still grinding.

Still *playing football*.

SUNDAY

The heart wants what it wants. I watch misty-eyed as the actual Broncos beat the actual Chargers in San Diego, and the five horses I have in the race perform beautifully. Demaryius, C.J., McmAnus, B-Marsh 2, and the Denver defense shut down the

Chargers 17–3. The Broncos' defense is the real star here—has been all year long.

The Sleeve's season may be over, but for the Broncos, the fun is just beginning. They say Peyton just got his cast off. Word on the tube is that he is working for a return to the field this season. But Brock Osweiler is undefeated in two games. Koob faces a difficult decision if Peyton becomes healthy enough to take the field again this season. I wouldn't want to be there at [Insert Corporate Logo Here] Field when he does. If he throws an incompletion, the sky might fall right onto the field and crush everyone.

I also watch the Niners beat the actual Bears in Chicago. I started Jay. He scores poorly: 4.08 points. I do not care. Jay is part of this team. He got us two Bunny Rings the last two years. He is a champion. But the 49er team win is aided by an excellent performance from quarterback Blaine Gabbert, who the experts tell us is a bad football player.

I also start Vincent Jackson—my guy. My little playbook stunt worked, as Vinnie got back on the field and scored well for the Sleeve in back-to-back weeks. Finally, I saved my best cry for B-Marsh. He catches 12 passes for 131 yards and a touchdown: 40.10 points. When I watch him play it feels like I'm playing again. I remember being on the field with him—working together. I know his movements, his body language. He needs the ball. Throw it to him *now*! Because he will catch it, which he does, and lifts the Jets over the Giants in overtime.

Tough times don't last; tough people do.

As long as I'm playing fantasy football with my derelict friends, I will have these men on my team. I will choose with my heart. Or else what good is it to have one?

Bunny Sleeve wins the last game of the season: 177–170. The heart knows best.

Final record: 5-8.

MONDAY

Team meeting.

I'm standing at the podium, scanning the room: the eighteen faces of football truth. B-Marsh is on the far right, like always. Jay, Pierre, Vincent, C.J., Demaryius, Jason Witten, Martellus, Alshon, McmAnus. Geez. They're all waiting for me to say something—something meaningful. I have failed them. I know that now. Oh, but it felt so right in August! Every one of my picks—felt just right. I had a winner and I knew it. No doubt. And yet here we are, confronting the dead body.

"Hmmm, guys, geez . . . well—where do I even start? It wasn't long ago that we were sitting in here . . . fresh as a Subway sandwich, ready to take on the world. But things change. Time goes by so fast, and so slowly, all at the same, well, *time*. Time makes fools of us all, boys. We aren't just humans, ya know; we are also people. The thing is . . . I can't . . . well . . . Guys, if you look in the mirror, and you see a sparrow, are you then a sparrow? . . . Look, I know y'all are hurting. I know you're tired. I know you're horny. . . . Sometimes failure is a blessing, because in failure we discover that we are more than the number on our back. We are more than the logo on our helmet. We are more than our *numbers*."

I hold up a calculator, then throw it against the wall behind me. It crashes to the floor in one piece.

"Yeah . . . I chose you guys because of the numbers. But there's more to it. I chose you guys with my *heart*, because I believed in you as *men*. I still do. But for some of you—I'm just going to say it—this is the end of the line. Okay? Your football careers are *over*. For you guys, I want to leave you with this: your new life begins today. *Life!* Ever heard of it? Of course you haven't! You've been in here! Look, life is your new struggle, fellas. And you must attack it with the same courage that you used out there on the football field. Football is easy, guys. Life is hard. I won't be out there with you in the real world telling you what plays to run. You're on your own now. So face it down, men. Face down the beast within. Don't turn from it. Or you will drag it around forever. Your identity has been suppressed for the good of this game—and I appreciate that you guys did that for this team—but out there . . . shit . . . out there you have to find out *who the fuck you are*. And let me help you out a little bit, just in case you get frustrated and forget. Football did not make you great. You made football great. *You!* You're some *badass motherfuckers,* boys. You hear me? Because to make it in *here*, to have the careers you did, you gotta be special: real fucking special. And that specialness is not confined to the game of football. That's not *who you are*. So find out who that guy really is, all right? Follow your nose. Use the money you earned in here to fund your search for your *self* out there, wherever it may take you. Believe me, you've got all the time in the world. Do yourself a favor and don't look at the clock. The clock is no longer your friend. Football fucked your sense of time forever, boys. You can exist in eternity during a six-second football play. It's going to be hard to duplicate that out there. It's going to feel like time is dragging on, spinning all around you while you sit still, unable to act on any thought. Don't let it take you down. Turn and face it. Face that which torments you and stick a knife in its neck!

"But I'm just gonna warn you. It's lonely down there. And you are going to have some hard days, some dark days, echoing into the abyss. You're going to think some crazy thoughts. Crazy thoughts are fine! They exist. That's life. But treat them like roaches and stomp on them. You are stronger than a roach! You are the giant!

But the hard truth here is that you must start from zero. Take the long view, dig your heels in, and trust your pain. Heartbreak and agony! Use it! Spray it on the walls! You got me? Spray it on the *fucking walls*!"

"For the rest of y'all—shit, what can I say? Don't do anything crazy this off-season. I guarantee I'll be seeing some of you in the summer. Just look for me . . . where the red fern grows.

Click!

I have a trapdoor in the meeting room, too.

The dogs love me this time of year.

WEEK FOURTEEN

BORN AGAIN

DENVER, COLORADO

"Christmas is right around the corner!"

Everything is right around the corner when you're going in circles.

It's funny how fast it turns.

The Sleeve is hibernating until August. Don't poke the bear. Don't feed the bear—unless you have some Movantik. But the actual football season is just now coming into focus. The Broncos lose to the Raiders at home with Brock Osweiler at the helm. Never lose to the Raiders at home!

There is a news report that comes out about Peyton. They call it "breaking news." The story is this: Peyton Manning will refuse a backup role once healthy and will demand to be released if he doesn't start.

The report is from "NFL Insider" Ian Rapoport, citing his source as "I'm sorry, did you say that you need a *source*?" There is a race to the bottom for dirt on the king. How many shovels did you bring?

SATURDAY

The holiday spirit moves and I move with it, from state to state. I'm following it home—to the rooftop where Santa walks and I'm going a few days early to attend a 49ers game at Levi's Stadium—Field of Jeans—with Ryno, who has season tickets. The Niners are in last place.

Super Bowl 50 is forty-nine days away, and will be played right here at Levi.

At what price comes the party?

I am going to find out. I'm doing this for *you*.

There is a Hyatt hotel right next to the stadium. I'll be staying here for two nights. My blue bag sings a hopeful entry song as I roll into the Hyatt's large lobby area: lots of seating and TVs turned to ESPN and college football. A twenty-foot Christmas tree, bulbously adorned, stands just inside the entrance. The woman at the front desk pecks at her keyboard with acrylic tips—click-click-click. *The weather outside is frightful, but the fire is so delightful.*

"Here you are, Mr. Jackson. Enjoy your stay."

Ding goes the elevator on the sixth floor. I step off whistling and key into room 616, drop my bag and open the drapes. There's Levi! It is oddly shaped for a stadium; not circular, or ovular, but more a half circle. From the front it looks like a large office building with a horseshoe behind it. The office building is parallel to the home sideline and it's where the rich people watch the game.

The horseshoe is for the peasants.

There are restaurants attached to the stadium that are open every day. Me, Ryno, and Wangs go to dinner at one of them— Bourbon Steakhouse. A stadium like this is not just for playing football games. It's a multifaceted moneymaker. Restaurants, banquet halls, shops: open for business all year long, and now gearing up for its moment in the spotlight when two teams not named the 49ers or Bunny Sleeve will duke it out for the top prize.

I'm going to Douchneyland!

Our sweaty waitress is trying to take our order, but Wangs is distracted. He is working on something on his phone, intently. He is on the StubHub website looking for tickets for tomorrow. Lots available.

"Should I pull the trigger?"

"Do it!"

"Should I? Boom!" he says and laughs and holds up the phone. "Done! Only a hundred and fifty apiece. That's a good deal, right?"

"Great deal!" says our waitress.

Wangs will be bringing Paho and sitting in the club level: that means access to the office building.

Our waitress tells us that we should come to the tailgate party tomorrow. They have it here at the restaurant. It's only five hundred dollars per person, she says, and it's a really good deal because it's all you can eat and drink and they open at eleven and stay open until the end of the third quarter. They get about 1,200 people at this tailgate.

"That's a lot of money," I say.

"Millions," she says, and squints her eyes; a devoted arbiter of the Sunday glut.

SUNDAY

I scrape the bourbon from my eyes and open the drapes again, looking across the wet, gray concrete parking lot to Levi. Game day! It is raining in Santa Clara. I am eating room service. Eggs and bacon taste better in my underwear.

Ryno texts: "Downstairs."

I put on pants and go down there—ding!—to find him sitting at a table in the lobby drinking a Bloody Mary—*red-rum-red-rum*—wearing a red 49ers sweatshirt and a gray beanie.

"Beany!" he calls out and holds up his spicy cocktail. Ryno calls me Beany.

It's 11 a.m. and already loud with hopeful drunks. Multiple NFL games already under way back east play on televisions and projectors aimed at open walls. People pose for photos in front of the Christmas tree. Sleigh bells are ringing. "Piano Man" pumps from the speakers and a brown-haired chick in a Bengals jersey and high-top Chucks does a spinning moon walk. The smell of hot oil and fried food wafts through and girls with butts walk by. The Bloody Mary looks good so I order one from Max, the overwhelmed emo waiter. It comes with a giant, leafy celery stalk sticking out of it, which I remove and place on the table. Max looks about to speak, cocks his head, scrunches his nose, and walks away.

Wangs and Paho arrive, Paho moving slowly and with purpose, Wangs zigzagging erratically, pretending to dry-heave as he looks around at the Sunday glut bubbling to life. They both order Bloody Marys, too: quadruple homicide.

If you go to an NFL football game, you will see many intoxicated individuals. You will see that alcohol is the main thing happening here. The disconnect between what it takes to be a professional football player and what it takes to be a professional football fan is striking. Drinking is the only gauge of your manhood here. Middle-aged men in goatees with potbellies look around with menacing stares. They are tough.

Just look at the name of the pro football players on the back of their jerseys.

The four of us played at Pioneer High School together. Ryno was a running back/defensive end. Paho was a lineman and Wangs was the quarterback. I was a receiver/free safety. None of us is wearing a jersey.

We are also in another fantasy football league together, less interesting to you, dear reader, as it did not have a destination draft. No bunnies, no fake-ass Brody Jenners: just a date and a time to log in. It would have been confusing for all of us to follow *three* leagues, but since we know Bunny Sleeve's fate, it would help if you all knew that I made the playoffs in this here league with my high school friends. And today I face Ryno in the playoffs. An extra bit of drama for a fun football day. Sunday Action! Wangs and Paho did not make the fantasy playoffs, and they couldn't care less about that because they have a much more direct approach to salvation. They share a bookie and a dream.

NFL football is hard to bet on. It is unpredictable because everyone is good. There are no bad teams in the NFL. Wangs has a membership to a pick-machine website that suggests which games to bet on based on the Vegas lines. It has a lock of the week (LOTW) every week that is supposed to be a sure thing. Easy money. But it hasn't been reliable the last few weeks, and if you follow someone's guess, and they guess wrong, then you lose your money. This week's LOTW is Chicago at +7 in Minnesota. Wangs trusted the machine and placed his bet. And now we're watching the Bears getting rolled by the Vikings, and he is yelling "fuck" just loud enough to make it fun.

The Niners are big underdogs today. I think they will win. They got crushed by Cleveland last week; humiliated, really.

And I believe in the professionalism of NFL teams to respond well after getting embarrassed. Since all of these teams are basically the same skill level, it becomes a battle of wills. And since every player knows that his job is on the line—especially in a shitty season—then they will find a way to right the ship. Plus the Bengals are without Andy Dalton, their starting quarterback, who broke his thumb. Also, I like the kill-the-narrative narrative, and the local story line is that the Niners are pathetic garbage. I want to believe otherwise. I make my case between bites of bloody celery but I do not convince either Wangs or Paho to take the Niners.

One of the morning games is between the Giants and the undefeated Panthers. The Panthers win, 38–35. Cam Newton throws five touchdowns and runs for 100 yards—another virtuoso performance—but the story here is Odell Beckham Jr.'s violent tantrum. Cornerback Josh Norman got in his head and Odell lost control, throwing punches, grabbing face masks, and taking cheap shots. This is exactly the reaction Norman was hoping for. Beckham has become the poster boy for the modern wide receiver. He is a freak athlete with crazy good hands and has received no small amount of praise for his excellent play. But the guys on the other side of the ball get paid, too. They are pros, too. And when they play against a guy who is getting fellated in the media, they want to teach him a lesson. They know about killing the narrative.

Consider Odell's narrative dead. He killed it himself. Football violence is constant. We become desensitized to it because it looks a certain way. There are rules. Stay inside the rules and you can murder someone on the field, for all anyone cares. But when you start swinging your fists and hitting people late, you draw attention to yourself and alert the conscience of the industry, which wants to see carnage look a certain way. The final-straw hit of the game-long scrap between Odell and Norman was a blindside cheap shot to the temple of Norman, who was standing next to a pile of players. The play was over. But not for Beckham, who was raging so fucking hard that all of the football-virtue rhetoric in the world couldn't stop him from attempting to end Norman's life. This is the line we are straddling. This is how close we are to losing it completely. We are training these boys to attack one another. We are gassing them up for assault.

Don't get skittish now. This is what you wanted.

We finish our drinks and walk to the stadium in a red-and-gold herd emitting alcohol fumes. Everyone is either drinking or drunk. "Drink Responsibly," says Bud Light, the NFL's official beer sponsor. How many would you like me to have, Mr. Light? One? Fifteen?

Ryno's season ticket seats are in the northwest section of the stadium—in the horseshoe. Wangs and Paho are in the luxury hotel with multiple levels of spacious concessions and bars and seating areas and nice bathrooms and artisanal food and girls with butts walking by. You have to show your tickets to be granted access to club-level amenities. Once you are inside, the vibe changes immediately. This separation is at the heart of some early Levi disenchantment. A football game is supposed to be the epicenter—fans sitting in a circle around a blazing campfire. Candlestick Park was a concrete circle of trust. Its concourses were tight and cramped. It wasn't *user friendly*, it was in service to the *game*.

Not the *experience*.

Ryno wisely advised Wangs to print out two sets of club-level tickets so that we can all take advantage of the *experience*. All you have to do is show them a club-level ticket to get into the private party. Who wants to stand outside with the peasants? We'll stagger our entry into the club level so as to not suspishify the ticket checkers. Wangs and Paho go in first while Ryno and I watch the coin toss from the concourse.

The crowd cheers the Jumbotron. Joe Montana and Ronnie Lott make their way to the fifty-yard line to flip the silver dollar. Joe's hair is silver, too, and Ronnie is walking a bit slower, but these men are legends. They have set an impossible standard, buoyed by the four Lombardi trophies in their indisputable past. They are a product of a bygone era, when heroes were not stripped down for our enjoyment. They existed for sixteen Sundays a year, plus the playoffs when we were lucky, which we always were.

Joe flips the coin into the air. As it rises and spins, it's anyone's game. The 49ers can win this thing! But the silver hits the green grass with a muffled clink and sets the game in motion. It's heads. Let's play. The Niners will receive the kick.

We show the lady our fake tickets and are granted entry. Just inside the door is a ten-foot-tall, thirty-foot-wide *YAHOO!* sign. Corporate amalgamations of gentrified tribalism. This is not a football game. This is Dave & Buster's. The concourse is a brand-new shopping mall! The stadium is empty and quiet, including half of the row that Wangs's and Paho's seats are in. We get twelve-dollar beers and sit down in the padded, comfortable chairs. One section over, on the other side of a retaining wall, sit the peasants in hard plastic chairs. Naked children, ribs exposed, lie in puddles as flies buzz around their heads and land in their eyeballs, which do not blink, only stare into the bitter sky, which looks about ready to open again.

Shaun Draughn carries the ball for a short gain. "Draughn strike!" yells Ryno.

The cheerleaders are dressed in Santa Claus outfits. I hear them pitter-pattering on my rooftop. I've been naughty. Four 49er fans in their late twenties sit in front of us. One of them has a homemade sweatshirt with a photo of 49ers head coach Jim Tomsula on the front that says, "Mediocre coach by day," and on the back is a photo of notorious porn star Ron Jeremy in a

Santa hat that reads, "Porn star by night." Heavy resemblance. We praise his shirt.

"We had a sign, too," he says, "but they took it away at the gate."

"Really?"

"Yeah, no freedom of speech at Levi."

"What did it say?"

"It was a picture of Donald Trump and it said *Make the Niners Great Again.*' I got it laminated and everything."

Laminated and everything! The mood is pessimistic. Collective expectations that everything will go wrong. And when you expect it to happen, well, you'll get what you want. The energy is low. The game is a sleeper. And I was wrong about the Niners. I thought they'd come out hot but they are uninspired. The game moves along at a slog. It is 0–0 into the second quarter and we get up for more beer. When we return, the seats we stole have been stolen by someone else, so Ryno and I head up to sit with the plebes.

Three law enforcement officials lean on a wall in the wide concourse area, wearing camouflage tactical gear and holding AR-15s, fingers on the triggers. Just in case some Bengals fan gets any funny ideas, which increases in likelihood as the Bengals score 21 unanswered points in the second quarter and go into halftime with a commanding lead.

There is a halftime ceremony to honor the Super Bowl–winning 49ers of yesteryear. Joe and Ronnie walk out onto the field holding the Lombardi trophy, flanked by Jerry Rice and John Taylor and Roger Craig and Harris Barton; the heroes of my childhood. They soak up the love. They know what it means, especially in this new context. As does Eddie DeBartolo Jr.—the owner of those Niners—who shows up waving on the Jumbotron and gets a standing ovation. Then the ceremony ends and half the fans get up to leave.

"Wow! Really? It's only halftime."

"They've been doing it all year."

We go back into the club level looking for televisions play-ing different games, so we can watch an entertaining contest. We don't find one so we settle on more booze—plenty of that around here—and sit along the window. A portly fella dragging his limp-legged friend sits him down next to us and asks us to keep an eye on him.

"He's drunk."

"Is he?"

This is amateur hour, emasculated American men seeking manhood by osmosis, hoping to gain access to their team's toughness by proximitous whiskey intake. These fuckers. I don't care who wins this game. I only want to teach these men a lesson about pain and violence. I only want them to hit the ground.

The game ends with a whimper. Niners lose. Bengals cover the spread. Wangs and Paho win money: lifelong Niner fans rewarded by their team's ineptitude. Back at the Hyatt we find seats at a long bar table in the crowded lobby. Fried food is or-dered. The booze is taking the wheel now. Best to just sit back and enjoy the ride. Let your better self lead, the one that doesn't think of tomorrow.

The one with a bottomless stomach.

The one with an endless bank account.

The one who fucks like a swordfish.

The immortalish man.

Wangs asks who I like in the late game. I like Arizona. I like them to win because I like what they are doing. I like their coach, Bruce Arians. I watched *A Football Life* on the NFL Net-work a few weeks ago and Arians was the feature. Most NFL coaches come from the same mold. The only way you get power in the NFL is to act like all of the other coaches. That's what I thought, at least, until I watched Arians's story. He is a contrarian. He does it his way. He wonders why coaches sleep in their offices and wake up at 4 a.m. to watch film. Football is easy, he says. Let's not make this complicated. Let's be human beings and play some fucking football. I like this man. I see why his team is responding to him.

I convince Wangs to take Arizona against Philly, which he does. He shows me on his phone how easy it is. "Look! Just press the button. Do it! Yeah!" He wants me to press it so I do. Now we are in this together. Arizona jumps out to a nice halftime lead, and Wangs redoubles his bet with a new adjusted halftime spread. There seems to be no limit to the number of bets, spreads, and odds that one can place wagers on. Arizona wins handily and Wangs wins a hefty purse, which enlivens his spirits, as do the spirits we are throwing down like water, charged to the room of course, and paid for by the advance to this book.

Sundays are for football.

Jesus wouldn't disagree.

MONDAY

Five days until his birthday and the holiday spirit moves up the 101 to San Francisco proper. But the spirit of the 49ers does not. I don't see it anywhere!

But let's not dwell on corporate logos during the most wonderful time of the year. Come now, ye faithful; come along, let's go. . . .

The holiday spirit moves through the pungent streets of Chinatown, in a flatbed truck full of dead pigs, on a conveyor belt of candy and sculptures and beads. It twists through Coit Tower and sloshes through the gutters of the Tenderloin. Santa hits the pipe. This is a stressful time of year for him.

The holiday spirit moves through an empty lot by the bay shore—formerly Candlestick Park—and on to a boardroom blueprint meeting in a shiny building in Silicon Valley. The holiday spirit moves through Hunter's Point, ghetto adjacent to Candlestick Lot, formerly buoyed by the Niners, now left for crunch by another marketing arm and bulldozer.

The holiday spirit moves through the rain-splashed streets of North Beach, cappuccinos and tiramisu and hotels with creaky wooden steps; forbidden love, fire-breathing whiskey-drinking night magicians fuck underneath a blanket of electric fog.

The holiday spirit moves under my feet, one step and then the next; walk it all away now. Fear is slow-footed. Lose it in the alley.

Jingle bells, Batman smells, Robin laid an egg. The Batmobile lost its wheel and Joker got away.

The Joker got away.

FRIDAY

I couldn't come home for Christmas in the NFL. We had practice. We had a game to get ready for. We had playoffs. We were bigger than the American social pact. We were bigger than Jesus. We were living on the moon!

Now I'm back on earth and watching my eight-year-old niece open gifts. She is happy here, in the sweet present. When does the switch flip? It still smells the same in this house. Smells the same outside. Same trees. I've climbed all of them. My blood still stains the concrete. My handprints are still on the top of that lamppost. The scars are still on my head. The street is the same. But something else is different.

The cosmic joke: I walk the streets that gave me wings and each step hurts. I focus on symmetry. I focus on straddling the line on the sidewalk. I can't do it. I'm off-kilter. My ankle is still gunked up and my back and hips are twisted. One leg is an inch longer than the other.

I fall asleep that night with the blue/green/red Christmas

lights cutting through the slits in the blinds and washing my bed in candy-cane nostalgia. Rich food and wine and sugar; my mind is aslosh. My weakened spirit lets the doubt in.

Again I dream of football.

(I wonder why!)

This time another NFL team: the Carolina Panthers. I was welcomed with open arms by Cam Newton and given a seat at the table, some dinner table at some restaurant and the team was gathered around and everything was taken care of. I felt like I was a part of something special, truly, making preparations and plans to keep this train rolling. My advice was sought after. Players and coaches were asking me questions. I was a missing piece, or something. They wanted me around, thought I could really help them going forward. Then we found ourselves out on the practice field.

Football stuff.

Ah, yes! I know this feeling. These smells. These sounds.

"Jackson! Get in there!" I reach down for my helmet and there are dozens of helmets on the ground. I sift through them looking for mine and start to panic. I can't find it! Where's my fucking helmet? It's nowhere. The moment passes. Someone else jumps into the huddle and I wake up in a sweat, in the same bedroom that used to be pasted with 49ers posters and hope.

The memory is sweet.

Now is salty.

Now is an acquired taste. Now is holding a clipboard and a lab coat, talking in stern whispers about *mortality* and *liability* and *chronic traumatic encephalopathy*.

Concussion opened today to mixed reviews. Who cares, though, really? It's a trick. Hollydouche is soaking it up. Will Smith is soaking it up. Bennett Omalu is soaking it up. Will gets a Golden Globe nomination. The NFL chooses to ignore it outright. The NFLPA is using it as an "awareness" tool.

Awareness of what? That their source of income is a brain killer? Sony is allowing NFL players and their families to see the movie for free, an incentive to watching their lives flash before their eyes.

You're only a few short years away from *this*.

Merry fucking Christmas!

SUNDAY

Los Angeles International Airport: I await an overstuffed bag at carousel 2 among a miserable collection of fidgeting humans. Christmas looks different on the back end.

Heavy is the head that wears the beanie. Shots fired at an ailing Peyton Manning, this time a report about human growth hormone (HGH). Al Jazeera made a documentary about doping in sports, which included a story about HGH being shipped to his house under his wife's name back in 2011. Now Peyton has to play along. ESPN came running to the Broncos' headquarters' toady to ask him the *tough questions*. They did the interview in the newly constructed indoor practice field. That field did not exist when I was there, six years ago. It was part of an entire new addition of a full indoor practice field with offices and two locker rooms and all kinds of awesome new facilities. They are constantly upgrading their facilities. The state loves them unconditionally. Marijuana is legal. The women are friendly. The air is clean. Their coach used to play there. Marijuana is legal. The *Most Famous Bronco Ever* runs the team. The stadium is righteous. The local economy is on fleek. And probably most important, the ownership and management supports its players and wants only for them to succeed, and doesn't overreact responding to bullshit Al Jazeera reports.

So anyway, Peyton took some time away from his rehab and throwing session to tamp down the HGH hullabaloo. He looked at the microphone in disgust, saying "all the right things" through a clenched jaw. The reporter pressed on with queries about his wife, who was implicated in the story as the named recipient of multiple HGH shipments—apparently as the cover for her junkie husband's illegitimate path to neck health.

You think HGH made Peyton Manning a good football player? If you say yes, ask your doctor about Movantik.

I t is the last Sunday of the regular season and I'm in Las Vegas, sitting in the Wynn's casino sports book, drinking a Corona, eyeballs swollen from the Super Sunday glut. Checkout was at noon. It's 1 p.m. My flight is at 4 p.m. I'm hurting after two nights here. My friend Alan plays piano for Michael Bublé and had a show at the MGM Grand on New Year's Day. We came, we saw, we spent a lot of money.

"Behold the Carnival of Flowers!" says Steve Wynn, distracting me from my agony. Steve Wynn is the blind magician, the desert hypnotist. Me be the willingly deceived.

Every NFL game is on TVs encircling the bar and huge screens line the sports book gambling area. Also every horse race, tennis match, golf game, and chess tournament is playing below the betting odds. Form a line at the front of the big smoky room to place your bet. Or just sit here and drink beer like me, and squint at all the screens. Constantly changing camera angles and slow-motion replays flicker like a snake across the room. Statistics flash in bubble font and announcers guffaw. Viagra and Toyota and Doritos interrupt the action. The American Man sips his poison and glances at the losing ticket in his hand, hoping it had a change of heart. Gamblers high-five out-of-towners after touchdowns by midwestern teams, then light another cigarette, which is sucked out and replaced quickly by Steve Wynn's trademarked candy-filtered oxygen.

"Yay, *Chiefs*!" shouts a guy from Kansas.

The Broncos are playing the Chargers at home. I'm watching them silently. They are not scoring touchdowns. Brock's hold on the starting spot is slipping: HGH reports and plantar fascia and little experts be damned!

Emmanuel Sanders has a long catch and run that ends with a fumble. "Do your fucking *job*!" yells a middle-aged man on steroids and leans back on the couch. He puts his arm around his curly-haired girlfriend. She emits a raspy laugh and looks at her pack of cigarettes. The waitresses scuttle about with sad eyes and happy teeth. This is so depressing. I do not want to leave.

But one must leave Vegas. One must always leave Vegas. There will be no absolution here. It is always incomplete. You cannot take these flowers with you. You can only smell them. You leave empty-handed no matter what. Now wheel your dirty bag out the gold-plated front doors, get in the cab, and go!

Popeye's breasts grease up my fingers at the airport; crunch, smoosh, slurp. I swallow and try not to vomit, then stand bleary-eyed on the periphery while the Southwest lines fill up. *C* stands for *Center*, which puts me between two probably humans. I don't know for sure because I do not look in their eyes. I am in a movie. When I land in L.A., my phone tells me that the Broncos have won 27–20. Looks like Brock came around after all! That's going to make it a tough call for Coach Koob in the playoffs. Who do you start: the young gunslinger or the old peashooter?

But back at home I see the highlights of their victory, and see that fate has been sealed. It wasn't Brock who led the Broncos to victory. It was Old Man River, suited up but not playing, until the Broncos found themselves down by ten. Brock was struggling.

"Can you go?" Coach asked Old Man River.

"If you need me," said the steely-eyed vet. Koob gave him the nod and Peyton took the field and led the comeback. This is how coaches help win games. Peyton has mojo in the tank: full reserves, ready to burn. Koob sees it. Koob sees everything.

The Broncos secured home-field advantage and a first-round bye with the win. Denver is Peyton's once again.

And now it is Super Bowl . . . or *death*.

B ack on Peyton's trail, I rehire Tracy. But this time I'm not going to screw it up with her. I'm going to be someone she can trust. She walks in and sits down.

"Coach, I just want to thank you for this opportunity. Ever since I was a little girl, I've wanted to be a part of this game. I've—"

"Please, Tracy, please. Tell me about your personal life. How is that going?"

"Excuse me, Coach?"

"Yeah . . . you . . . your . . . boyfriend, right?"

"It didn't work out," she says.

"Oh yeah? Why not?"

"Well, do you want the truth?"

"Of course, Tracy, please!"

"Okay. Well, I was working at this other job—this job I cared a lot about—and it had taken over my life, but I didn't resist. No . . . I didn't resist it. And it was horrible and great all at the same time. I loved what I was doing, Coach, but eventually it started to take its toll on me. It started to wear on me. And the truth is—the truth is that the whole time I thought that I was falling for my boyfriend, I was really falling for the man who wouldn't love me . . . the man I'd loved all along . . . the man of my dreams, the man I *worked* for, the man who—"

"Tracy!" I cry. "It's me! It's me! The man you love! I . . . I . . . I love you, too!"

Tracy loosens her shoulders and sinks a little in her seat and starts to laugh, slowly at first, then harder and harder until she almost can't breathe. Then she licks her lips and holds up her left hand, which displays a modest diamond.

"C'mon, Coach. Only the players forget being cut. I was just fucking with you. I'm engaged."

"But, I—"

"Not gonna happen, Coach. But I still believe in this team. Let's go win a Super Bowl."

PLAYOFFS

NUMBERLESS LEGENDS

DENVER, COLORADO

At the top of the last long escalator, Jake says hello to another sweet old Bronco lady—by now we've spoken to several. She gives him a hug, too. I'm just following him. Everyone knows Jake Plummer here. Then we march on around the bend and stop in front of the door to the suite above [Insert Corporate Logo Here] Field. The game is about to start.

"Ready to meet Roger?"

"Fuck yeah."

We shake hands and walk into suite 411, Commissioner

Goodell's suite, to watch the Broncos play the Steelers, smelling like the truth.

Ha! Yes, that Commissioner Goodell. The real life one. Not the one who came to the Turtle House. Let me back up.

For this book to have any jizz to it, it needs *action*. Scenes. Characters. Poop. And so I have embraced NFL football this season. I have thrown myself into it. And I'm pulling my friends in with me. This game is one of those scenes.

And so we had planned to go to this playoff game all week. Six of us got regular tickets—Me, Jake, his father-in-law, my old Bronco buddy Charlie Adams, and a few other friends. Then a few days ago I was staring at my computer again, eyeballs crossing again, jumping, double-crossing—when Jake called me and said he was invited to go to Goodell's suite for the game.

"Whaaaat? Cool!"

"Wanna join me?"

"Fuck yeah!" I said.

Roger Goodell is the archvillain in the modern football saga. But I've also been told that he is a nice guy. Ha! Yeah right! How can he be *nice*? He is the slimy politician. He is the snake in the grass. He is the prison warden. He is my oppressor. He does not care if I live or die. I am going to tell him what I think. I'm going to make sure he listens.

I went through a few old bags of Broncos gear this morning, looking for some clothes to help me blend in at the game. No luck. Everything is way too big now. Who was the monster that wore these? This beanie will work, though. It's an old badge of honor from my meat-grinding days. It says "DBST" on it in orange block letters—Denver Broncos Special Teams—and was given out to players who had a particularly good game on special teams: recognition for the unrecognized.

Charlie's girlfriend drops four of us off on the edge of the stadium's south parking lot. iPhones and a description of the red flannel Jake is wearing lead us to his tailgate: a small grassy area between a multicolored industrial building under the Colfax overpass: chairs and barbecues and fans and coolers. Jake's truck is backed in and he stands in a circle with his wife's dad and a few other friends. There's a group of Broncos fans next to him, everyone mingling, happy to be drinking with real meatheads.

Cans get snapped and sandwich trays go around; sweet and low clouds float over the sea of Broncos fans, mooding themselves for the biggest home game in a while. One win and you're in the AFC Championship game. But the Broncos are playing the Steelers, who seem to have always had our number, especially in the playoffs. We lost to them here in the AFC Championship in 2005. Jake was our QB. I was standing on the sidelines in sweats, chewing sunflower seeds.

But I was also here in 2011—in the stands—when Tim Tebow threw a touchdown to Demaryius Thomas on the first play of overtime to beat the Steelers in the first round of the playoffs—crucifying the narrative.

Sit back and watch the wobbly truth in flight.

Sit back and watch the immortal man gallop over curbs and under branches to snare the duck thrown by five well-intentioned delicate fingers on the other side of the grassy knoll. I spit on my hands and rub them together and sling one back. It cuts through the crisp mountain air like a bullet. No pain. No worries. Only movement. Only the sweaty moment. It catches me up in all things. I feel the blood tubing through me and launch another pearl, then go back to the cooler.

"Beers?"

"Sure," says the girl leaning into the moment with dark hair and black stretchy pants. I hand her a Mama's Little Yella Pils and hand one to myself and lift the tab. *Crack.*

"DBST?" she says as she opens the beer. "What's that?"

"Denver Broncos Special Teams."

"Like, special classes? Short bus?"

"Sort of."

The game is about to start. People are moving in blue-and-orange droves toward the stadium. We pack up the truck and join the crowd: buzzing orange, happy blue smiles, and keg cups crumpling. Sweet green and smoking meat clings to fabric and hangs in the air.

Near the front of the stadium where the bottles neck, Jake and I split off and head to our special entrance on the east side of the stadium. The air is cold. People are bundled up. But the sun is pushing through some early suggestions of snow. There will be nothing falling from the sky today—only the sky itself, should Peyton throw an interception.

The VIP entrance line is long. I follow Jake at an angle along a metal barricade and up near the door. Security notices Jake and waves us in front of a nonchalant collection of joyous individuals. Sundays are football. Jesus would agree. Jesus *does* agree! There he is ahead of us on the escalator, holding a chalice and dressed warmly in neutral colors. Jesus does not care who wins. He just wants to see a good game.

We head up three separate escalators—old-lady hugs at every checkpoint. It feels good to be treated so well in a palace like this. And now here we are, standing in front of the commissioner's door. Well, let's go meet this asshole! We walk in. It's a normal luxury box—two rows of ten seats up front against the glass, then up a few steps to a common area with tables and food set up. There is a private bathroom in the back near the entrance. We take off our coats and hang them on the rack.

Roger is not here but his wife, Jane Skinner, is. Well, this should be great! I can only imagine what kind of woman would be married to the *commissioner* of the N . . . F . . . L! She must be the epitome of . . . kindness. Roger, she says, went to another suite real quick to say hello to Archie Manning, who just had a few new hips put in. But here, meet my daughters, Jane says, and introduces me to her twins. Oh, great, *twins*! Of course, they are going to be completely . . . sweet and nice and polite.

Archvillain Goodell: family man.

Also in the suite are Blank and Blank, friends of the Goodell's and owners of a local telecommunications company. Two of their adult daughters are present—beautiful and well fortified with sparkly diamonds on ring fingers. The claim to one of those diamonds is also present, sitting in one of the front-row seats with his phone propped up on the windowsill, streaming a college basketball game.

Rod Smith is here with his twenty-one-year-old son. Former Broncos safety Dennis Smith is here with his wife. Dennis is a local legend, still with a football body and smiling affectionately. Also there are a few more folks, personnel, strangers, somebodies. The names! The names! They don't stay in my brain.

Roger returns to the suite, greets his wife warmly, then meets all of the new strangers, including your narrator. I know who Roger Goodell is. If he knows who I am, he doesn't show it. Books like mine don't end up on the desks of men like him. Ideas like mine don't get considered at meetings with men like Roger. Or maybe that's just another narrative that needs a bullet. We shake hands: the smallest of talk. This is not a political rally. This is a playoff game, and it's about to begin.

I fill up my plate with slices of a well-cooked roast, a variety of artisanal salads, and a roll. Then I open the fully stocked refrigerator underneath the counter with the heated metal food trays and grab two Budweisers, and take my seat to watch the football fly. There will be no deception here today. Big Ben Roethlisberger is nursing a bad shoulder that was pile-driven by a bloodthirsty Vontaze Burfict last week. Burfict went full pyscho just like Odell Beckham—frothed up by the industry, then aimed at the temple of his rival. The cannon exploded. Vontaze is the cannonball. Don't blame him for the carnage.

You lit the fuse.

Eating food and watching the game and chatting with old friends and new strangers: I thought this room would feel like a Secret Service meeting. But it just feels like humans enjoying another football game. The *game*. The game is the powerful thing here—everyone in awe of what is happening on the field.

Well, everyone but what's-his-nuts watching basketball on his phone.

The real-life game in front of us is a low-scoring affair. Defense reigns. The Broncos' offense sputters along, controls the clock, a few bursts, nothing doing, punt-punt: whatever. Keep it close and anything can happen, but still. I hear the boos coming up from down that way, and some more coming up from over there.

Boo? Booing what? This is the NFL *playoffs*. They are booing a lack of offensive perfection. But it's of no consequence, because there is something else at work here. There is the *organism*: vital, and now complete.

One end slackens; the other end stiffens. One side lurches, the other side compensates. One side vomits, the other side eats. The Denver Broncos have reached a moment in their season—this very moment right now—when the truth of what they are becomes very plain, and it took this long for everyone to get it. To get that one side depends on the other; that they are the *same*; that a lower offensive output is the only recipe for maximizing the potential of the defense, which knows what must be done and rises to the occasion. And in the end, after a forced fumble by the Broncos' defense, it's Old Man River who leads the winning drive: dink dink dunk. Touchdown! Broncos win!

Roger and Company duck out early to beat the crowd while Jake and I watch the clock run out on the Broncos' win. Great game. Great atmosphere. Great food. Great fridge with much beer leftover. Great pockets on the inside of my jacket. Great to be alive and weighed down by hope.

Stop. I have to piss.

Lighter again, we meet Charlie and folks back at the truck and the herb comes around and I take a nice pull, exhale, and feel the fuzzy spots in my brain expand.

We all hop in Jake's truck, three of us smashed back in the cab behind chairs and dog toys and garments, the rest in front. I laugh, yell something to the guys up front. They don't hear me. Jake drops us off at Charlie's apartment and drives back to Boulder with his father-in-law, while we storm into Charlie's place and ride the Orange Dragon until it coughs and sputters and I fall heavy on a dirty futon—my old futon, actually; squeak squeak squeak. Look ma, I'm asleep.

TUESDAY

SAN FRANCISCO, CALIFORNIA

Now, you listen here, I ain't no journalist, but I figured I had better come and see this NFL season end in person, for the sake of *Fantasy Man*. Because God obviously wants me here, and wants the Sleeve here, too.

God is a bunny.

The Broncos beat the Patriots last week to earn a spot on the field at Levi's Stadium on Sunday against the heavily favored Carolina Panthers. But the Super Bowl is about so much more than that itty-bitty football game they play down in Santa Clara. There's a tornado of cash coming to San Francisco. So come on! Let's head into the storm.

Back in the Loin, I step over a fresh turd. Only an edge has been flattened. There are a few areas of the city dedicated to the promotion of Super Bowl 50, as well as massive decals covering high-rise buildings throughout the city. One of the promotions is "Super Bowl City," a cordoned-off section of about four or five square blocks at Market Street and the Embarcadero. As you approach Super Bowl City on foot along Market Street, you encounter a series of televisions built into small cranes with SB50 logos hanging out over traffic, playing clips from old Super Bowls. There is security at every one of these themed promotional art installations because people have been vandalizing them. Some folks are pissed about the Super Bowl. The setup has been massive, redirecting traffic routes all week and shutting down areas that aren't otherwise closed.

Nothing pisses off Californians more than redirected traffic.

Upon entering SBC your first reaction will be confusion. What is it? you'll ask. It's hard to tell. It looks like one long commercial break. Every corporate sponsor found an interactive way to cross-promote with the NFL's SB50 brand using themed booths adorned with football-shaped logos. People are posing for selfies in front of the logos. The cops with AR-15s seem friendly. After Commercial Row there is a big open space with stages set up and the TV networks broadcasting live behind glass walls. Fans stand outside looking in at the aging Hall of Famers preparing for a taped segment about Peyton Manning's possibly cryptic retirement message hidden in his stock answers to his media-day questions one day ago. I imagine this open area with stages and corporate carnival games and fried food and Bud Light booths will be very crowded later in the week. I don't see a Movantik booth anywhere. BYOM.

In order to clear the space for this NFL theme park, the city has apparently pushed the homeless to a predesignated section of the city a few miles away, underneath a freeway overpass, creating a tent city. This is one of the things that people are pissed about—*where* the homeless must be homeless, not necessarily that they are homeless.

The local disenchantment with the corporate takeover is understandable. San Francisco's heartbeat has always been anti-authoritarian, anticorporate. The sentiment hardened during the cultural revolution of the mid-1960s, which has colored our ideals for five decades; reality be damned. But even in that magical moment, buses packed with middle Americans started cruising down Haight Street to gawk at the hippies like monkeys at the zoo. And by the early seventies, it was finished. The eulogy was carved on Charles Manson's forehead.

Game over.

This shall not be duplicated.

Better to let Hunter S. Thompson tell it:

> There was madness in any direction, at any hour. If not across the Bay, then up the Golden Gate or down 101 to Los Altos or La Honda. . . . You could strike sparks anywhere. There was a fantastic universal sense that whatever we were doing was *right*, that we were winning.
>
> And that, I think, was the handle—that sense of inevitable victory over the forces of Old and Evil. Not in any mean or military sense: we didn't need that. Our energy would simply *prevail*. There was no point in fighting—on our side or theirs. We had all the momentum; we were riding the crest of a high and beautiful wave. . . .
>
> So now, less than five years later, you can go up on a steep hill in Las Vegas and look West, and with the right kind of eyes you can almost *see* the high-water mark—that place where the wave finally broke and rolled back.

Rolled back, indeed. Hunter put a shotgun in his mouth a few years ago, so he can't join us. But if he were here today, walking along the Embarcadero, I wonder what he'd think about the Bay Area he knew. I wonder what he'd say about Super Bowl 50. I wonder if anyone would listen.

I doubt they would. There's a new wave rising in San Francisco. Surf's up!

WEDNESDAY

K-9 homeland security cops with assault rifles canvas Larkin between Eddy and Van Ness, searching for a perp—real or imagined. Ten of them are manning corners, tight-lipped and taut-necked, SUVs parked on the sidewalk. I walk by and nod at the old cop with the big gun and the dark sunglasses.

Did he see me? Does he *know*?

Ryno is on his way and then we're going to Radio Row, which is a collection of all Super Bowl media in one room. You need a credential to get in. And you need a media connection for the credential. Ryno was my connection. He has acted as local publicist and has set up multiple interviews with Bay Area radio shows by contacting them online, knowing they'll be looking for guests during the weeklong smorgasbord of *blah-blah-blah*.

You come to Radio Row if you have something to promote, or if you have a message you want to get out, or if you want someone to offer you a job. You will recognize people here from TV. You will see radio people whom you usually only hear. You will see football players in street clothes. You will see old-timers, Hall of Famers, Pro Bowlers, pro *bowlers* (bowling) promoting new memoirs (*Spare Me* and *Split Personality*). You will see well-dressed women in modest heels moving purposefully through the room. They are used to dealing with big-egoed mandolescents. They endure it in order to work in a field they love—like Tracy.

You will see old friends from Denver. You will see your old

agent, Ryan, in the Sirius XM section. You will attempt to walk in and talk to him and will be stopped by a guy with a Sirius polo shirt and stick in his ass.

"Do you know someone in here?"

"Yes. My agent is right there."

"Oh . . . o . . . kay . . . go ahead."

You will tell your agent that he is going to be in your book again.

"What part?"

"This part!"

You will see Dana White, UFC president, doing interviews to promote *his* brand: America's Other Bloodsport. Football and fighting are similar; it's true. But they tend to capture different cross-sections of American machismo. Football is more rhetorical, tactical, and militaristic. Football is not about you; it's about the guy next to you. In mixed martial arts (MMA), the guy next to you is the one trying to kill you. You will see a look in Dana White's eyes that can only be taken for envy for the *institution* of the NFL—and the landslide of money it creates.

Jesus H. Beanstock, this place is exhausting. Stay focused! It will bear fruit. The Canadian peach standing next to me in flowing ensemble is ripe on the vine. She's contemplating a career in broadcasting, she says. She doesn't know much about the NFL, she says. Many people here will be eager to help her.

"Listen for the twenty," I tell her.

"What does that mean?" she asks.

"My book drops in September."

I keep moving. We came here for a reason: *heavy self-promotion.* We are here to *sell books.* Old books, new books, future books. Go on the radio or TV or whatever you can and promote your *brand.* Put your theories to work. The way you kill this narrative is by making your brand *no brand.* If you build it, they will come. If you tear it down, they will come harder.

No brand is really *brand strengthening* because of course I played in the NFL: that will never leave me no matter what. The way I set myself apart is by speaking my personal truth, but the tongue takes time to warm up. The throat, in conjunction with the lips and the teeth—and don't forget the mind! Lean into the microphone. Look them in the eye. Think about the question you are asked. Try not to open the canned answer. Channel the moment! Say what needs to be said!

But the first interview is choppy. It's with a stand-in host on a show I'm unfamiliar with. The young kid with the beard asks me questions. I stutter. I'm a baby deer. There are too many people walking around! It's distracting. Too much eye candy. Radio is ear candy! Give them ear candy!

"So are you saying that the . . ." he posits.

I don't know what I'm saying. I'm studying his beard. It's an orangish brown color and seems full of thickets and weeds, and is shaped like a mound of mashed potatoes one has given up on eating. He finishes his statement with an inflection that indicates conclusion, and I pry my attention from his facial pubes in time to make a salient point one beat before the sponsors must be paid. *Aaaaand, scene!* He cuts to commercial and the interview is over.

Next up is San Francisco radio guy Damon Bruce: local provocateur. I'm on in a few minutes. Ryno and I are talking to the producer. Damon is on with a current Raiders defensive player—a massive man in a tiny white folding chair. Two chicks with shiny skin and expensive bags stand behind him talking about nannies. The producer asks me what I've been working on, what I want to talk about.

"Whatever. Anything."

"I saw the *Real Sports* piece," he says. "Wanna talk about medical marijuana?" An HBO *Real Sports* medical marijuana piece that I was in recently re-aired with an update.

"Sure."

The show is on a commercial break. Producer tells Damon what we can talk about.

"Cool," says Damon. "How about you come in a segment early and we can all be on the air for a bit. Is that cool?" Damon asks the Raiders guy.

"Sure," he says.

"Cool, we're going to talk about medical marijuana. Is that all right?"

Raiders guy stiffens up.

"Ummm." He looks back to his girl.

"Medical *marijuana*?" she says. "No, no, no, we can't do that. We better go."

"No, you're good," I say. "I'll wait until you guys are finished before I come on."

She looks at me disgusted and turns back to her friend. *Protect the Shield!*

The interview with Damon goes well. As much as I rail against the willful ignorance of NFL-related media, it's really a *national television* problem. Local radio guys are typically very receptive to a contrarian's discussion on NFL issues. They may not agree, but they'll hear you out. After all, they make a living by killing the narrative! They are old guys talking sports for a living!

As I'm walking around looking at the lights and cameras, a security guard stops me. Must be in a restricted area again.

"Man, I have to stop you real quick. I saw you on *Real Sports* and, man, I agree with what you're doing. I just have to shake your hand."

"Wow, thanks, man."

"For real, I had a bad shoulder injury and they gave me

OxyContin, morphine, everything. I was laid up in bed for a *year*, man, turning into a zombie. I was in a bad place. Finally I started smoking some weed instead and I got my life back, man. Off the pills and out into the world again in like a month. My wife said, 'Why you smoking weed, baby?' And then your piece came on, and I watched it like five times, man, and I said, 'Baby, come here, watch this!' So I just wanted to say thanks, man. Keep doing what you're doing."

We hug and I continue on. That's the good shit. The proof in the pudding. That single encounter will fortify me for the next decade to dive deeper into this, knowing that the truth does not exist in a vacuum, even though it sometimes feels that way.

Personal truth becomes universal truth if you speak it.

I find several clusters of Denver media, old friends of mine, looking for guests, too. They give me the headset and I jump in. The most obvious subject is the Super Bowl itself. Despite their hope that their home team will win, the six-point spread favoring 17-1 Carolina has most of these objective journalists picking against the Broncos. *Six-point favorites!* The money is coming in heavy on the Panthers. They are unstoppable. They've put up monster numbers on everyone, including their last two playoff opponents.

Stomp! Stomp! Stomp!

The Broncos are good and all, but this is the Panthers' year and this is Cam's team. In the two weeks that have led up to Sunday's game, the media has undertaken a Cam Newton character study. Troubled past, redemption, busting the mold, dancing too much, scaring white America, having fun with his homies, throwing touchdowns, running for touchdowns, smiling on the football field, putting a towel over his head, evoking his blackness, owning his likeness, breaking down walls, winning football games. Cam has taken it all on his shoulders. This is his moment. This game is about *him*.

Meanwhile, on Peyton's side, the narrative amounts to four hundred sneaky ways to get him to admit that he's done, that he can't go anymore, that he is retiring. It is the past versus the future: but what about *now*?

The juice is Carolinian.

But the milk is in Denver.

"So who do you got in the game?" asks Les Shapiro, long-time Denver sports radio guy.

"I got the Broncos," I say.

"Really?"

"Yeah . . . I think they're going to roll."

"Wait, they're going to *roll*?" interjects his cohost, Eric Goodman.

"Yeah . . . by two touchdowns."

"Wow! Well . . . we will see . . . but I don't know about that. The Panthers are too tough."

Kill 'em all!

After a few more interviews, my tongue is in a knot. Nothing more can be done today. You walk in circles looking for some action and you start seeing everyone over and over—hello, hello, hello again. It starts getting awkward.

Seventy percent of life is knowing when to leave.

So we leave, Ryno and I, and meet Razor around the corner at a local bar. Razor lives in the city. Several beers in and the blood starts pumping, and once the buzz comes on, the next step is *wings*. We head to the Phoenix hotel, where I'm staying, for a bit of help sprouting them, then we fly around the Tenderloin for a few hours, picking through garbage cans and lighting fires. But just as we're getting going, Ryno and Razor sheath their blades and leave me. It's a school night for them, but not for me.

So what's a man to do? A man who chases sweaty moments? A man who only wants to bleed?

I can only guess, because it all goes black again, right after I feel my two bicuspids turn to fangs and the buttons on my shirt pop out. The next thing I know, like last time, I awaken on the concrete. There are strangers stepping over me, rips in my clothing, a pounding headache. The difference is, in the Tenderloin, that's not out of place.

I stagger into my room and fall on the bed. I'd like to get some real sleep. But that ain't happening. The sun is coming up now. It always does that.

FRIDAY

"I'll be the one in all white;)," texted the Canadian, which provided an incentive for your narrator to give it one more try at Radio Row. I spent yesterday sleeping and writing. This thing is on its last breath.

The credential line at Moscone Center is long today; very long. Out the door and down the street. It isn't moving. I'm on the air in thirty-seven minutes. The weather is gorgeous: 70 and sunny. Sunny in San Francisco! Like Mark Twain said, the warmest winter I ever spent was a spring in Fort Lauderdale.

Lots of action at Radio Row today. People with lanyards and scrunched foreheads and phones in hand. I finally get my pass, run inside, and barely make an interview with Gary Radnich—Bay Area sports talk patriarch. I used to watch him on TV as a kid.

Ryno set this one up, too. He has been leading me from show to show—with purpose. I suggest a career change to him. He just laughs. *Gary & Larry* is the name of this show. They are nice guys, supportive of the local boy, happy to hear me out. I create these media wars in my head, but where is the opposition to this message? Not here. Everyone here is receptive to the other side of the coin. In fact, they long for it. They're starved for it.

Hey, look over there! It's Cuba Gooding Jr.! He is wearing sunglasses and a large colorful scarf that comes up over his chin. He is promoting his O. J. Simpson show. He is saying that he thinks O.J. has CTE. He's probably right. Funny thing is, no one really cares about CTE. That's what I'm realizing now. *Concussion* tanked. No one wants to take it on. No one wants to feel guilty about loving football.

And they shouldn't.

Aha! There she is. Dressed in all white just like she said. She seems happy to see me. She touches my arm. I feel special. She is excited, she says. She has had an amazing week. Everyone is so nice! But as she is telling me this, I feel heated eyeballs on me. Raging eyeballs! A bunch of radio guys behind her are cutting me to pieces. "Be gone with your beard and your backpack!" they say with beady little eyes. "She's mine!"

"Well maybe I'll see you tonight?" she says.

"Yeah, maybe—where are you going?"

"Might be going to the *Maxim* party."

"Nice."

"With Cuba."

"Gooding?"

"Jr."

Okay, one more interview. Let's do this and get the hell out of here. As I walk toward it, a crowd of people are coming at me, following someone famous through the room. Who are they following? We spot each other at the same time. It's B-Marsh.

"Buddy!"

He jumps up and down with that big warm smile and we hug. It's been a while: five years at least. My heart! In the flesh! The fans that have been following him look at me confused.

"You're crazy, Nate. I love what you've been saying!"

"*Me?* Man, I'm so proud of you. It's easy to do it from outside the bubble. You're doing it from *inside*!" In a few months, because of his excellent work on Showtime's *Inside the NFL*, B-Marsh will be nominated for an Emmy: the only active NFL player to ever be considered for the honor.

"We gotta go, B," says his handler.

"Okay, okay—let's go." We exchange numbers. He whispers the digits in my ear so the fans that are watching us don't hear it and start sending him unsolicited nude photos.

We hug again and he is off, the eager crowd following close behind, just like always. Go get 'em, Brandon.

Last interview and we can call this thing dead. The station is KOA in Denver, with hosts Andy Lindahl and Ed McCaffery, whom I played with in Denver, and another old teammate, Nick Ferguson, will be sitting in, too. I sit down and take the headset. Andy is looking at me weird. Come to think of it, Andy has been looking at me weird for several years now. His jaw is clenching. His lip is doing something funny.

"What's up, man? Everything good?"

"Yeah . . . it's fine . . . just . . . please, Nate. Don't cuss again, okay?"

"Huh?"

"You almost got me fired."

"*What?*"

Oh! I forgot about that. I was on his show once, years ago, just after my career had ended. I was thrashing mentally, unsure how to climb the tree and grab my coconut. I was riled up on air for some reason and I said, "Fuck!" There is a delay in radio, and the technician should have bleeped it. But he was new and was caught off guard and missed it. So he let a *fuck* through the wire and Andy took the heat for it and it shook him up pretty good: him being new at the station and all. And he has held it against me since. And now it all makes sense! I apologize to him and assure him that it won't happen ever again. He doesn't seem convinced.

The segment starts and I tell them about this book.

"What's it called?"

"Killing Peyton."

The record stops. Ed raises his eyebrows.

"Really?" he says. "Explain!"

I try. It goes poorly. The only thing I know for sure is that I like the title. So does everyone else—for now, at least. In a few months, the sales department will have a change of heart and kill *Killing Peyton*—afraid of ruffling the feathers of a bird in a cage in someone's basement.

Irony ain't what it used to be.

Either way, it provides for some good radio fodder and leads to a lively discussion about fantasy football and what it's doing to the fans. Andy is a die-hard Broncos fan; always has been. His whole family is that way. The *team*. You root for your *team*. But now it's all changing. He is trying to instill the team support in his kids, but he is fighting the tide.

Ed's son Christian was the runner-up for the Heisman Trophy as a running back for Stanford. There is fantasy football for college players, too.

People are making money off Christian.

Lots of it.

"How do you feel that people are profiting off of his performance?" asks Nick to Ed.

"Honestly, it's a bit unsettling. He can't even accept a free Warriors ticket to be honored at the game after the season he had."

Damn. It's all fucked up now.

Ryno and I shake hands with the guys and cut out into the street.

Goodbye, Radio Row!
See you next year.
I'll be the one in all white.

We are headed back to the Phoenix Hotel to meet the guys: Razor, Rocky, Twomp, and Origami Dan. We're going to hit a few Super Bowl parties tonight. As Ryno and I walk up through the Loin, discussing the solid week of radio work, a familiar shape appears next to us, hopping to the beat of the Super Bowl drum. Bunny! It's good to see you, friend. But why are you—oh! I know why you are here. To congratulate the winner of our fantasy season, Rocky.

We key into the courtyard and are greeted by shouts of joy from the fellas, who are on a good one already, milling around near the pool. Bunny hops right up to Rocky and gives him a big championship hug. Congrats, Champ! Better to be lucky than constipated.

We are going to a Gridiron Cannabis Coalition party at Hotel Zeta. We are on the list. Bunny is not. But no one notices him as we walk in and are handed a goodie bag. I peer inside: weed lotion and rolling papers and literature and other cannabis contraptions that I don't understand. The whole floor smells like weed. There is free food and an open bar. Bunny seems content. Mike, the lawyer who helps run the GCC, is on the microphone thanking everyone for coming. He is using a lot of industry terms that my friends find confusing, cross-referencing other cannabis companies that are involved somehow.

"This is so interesting," says Blanca, Razor's wife. "Everyone is so nice . . . but, well, what is it? I mean, what do they *do*?"

"No idea."

From there we go to another bar, down the street in SOMA. It's loud. Crowded. Bunny has a hard time getting a drink. After one beer we decide to head back to the Phoenix. As we walk down the alley—ten humans and one bunny—Twomp stops and cocks his head to the side.

"I'm gonna head home," he says, and motions back in the other direction, where he lives alone. We say goodbye to Twomp and continue on—all of us except Bunny. He's watching Twomp walk away. Something is passing between them. Bunny glances back at me with tears in his eyes, then turns away and hops down the alley toward Twomp, who is bathed in the soft yellow light of a streetlamp. He shoots an imaginary jump shot into the trash can just as Bunny catches up to him, and they both round the corner for good. Goodbye, Bunny. Goodbye, Twomp.

SATURDAY

Thirteen years ago, when I had yet to make an NFL roster, Wangs and I went to Leigh Steinberg's Super Bowl party at the San Diego Zoo. Leigh was the first of the big-name football agents, the man whom *Jerry McGuire* was based on. "Show me the money!" It was a cherry-popping, welcome-to-the-NFL party for me. We met two actresses on the way out and scheduled breakfast for the next morning. We hit a *Playboy* party later that night. I peed in empty beer bottles because the bathroom line was so long. The next morning Wangs couldn't make breakfast but I kept the date. It was an excellent meal. Wangs has always regretted skipping it. Perhaps he'll have another chance. I got us on the list for Leigh's party. Wangs is headed up from Los Gatos as we speak.

Thirteen years later and we are chasing the same dragon.

But I am tired . . . so tired. This week has been brutal, dear reader. Shit, the last four months have! I must level with you. This page may not look hungover but your author is. I have left you fairly early each night and have gone off in search of the sweaty moment. I'm happy to report that I have found it! A swan dive into the lake of fire!

"Fooouuur!" yells Wangs as he arrives in room 28 and finds me in shambles. He holds his four fingers up in the air and laughs. Our JV coach used to make us do that before the fourth quarter. I always felt stupid doing it. Like, why not do it for every quarter? Why just the fourth? By then it was too late anyway. We were 2-7 that year.

The day is gorgeous once again. The weather has complied. The city has risen to the occasion. My head is pounding. We walk through the Tenderloin toward Market and my spirits rise immediately, seeing these people sprawled out on the sidewalk, inches from death.

You know what? I'm quite all right, if I think about it.

We make it into the party, which is doubling as a silent art auction. The colors inside are blinding. Sundresses and sunshine; my retina feels detached; my cornea is swollen. My stomach is growling, but I press on. Nice dudes. Nice girls. The truth is, dear reader, dear friend—the truth is that I feel *comfortable* at these places. That's what has become of me. The booze is free and so is the food. No reason to leave. Where else would we go?

We have an enthusiastic circle of partygoers connected by three links in sports-people chains and it's fun untangling them. Adding to the stew is Jake Plummer, arriving with a beer in his hand and joined by his two older brothers and his childhood friend. The four of them come to every Super Bowl together. Jake gets paid to do appearances. It covers his trip and then some; then they go to the game. They've rented an Airbnb near the painted ladies at Alamo Park and have been spending time in the Mission District when not doing sanctioned stuff. The Super Bowl has a million parties and events, and half of the conversations at these places are about where everyone is going next, or went last night, or are going tomorrow. Jake has been telling me about the NFLPA's Legends Lounge. It's at the top of the Hilton just north of Market and it's awesome, he says. Crazy beautiful views of the city, empty up there, free drinks and food and everyone just hanging out. Jake is a legend.

Am I a legend?

Let's go find out. Wangs is in high spirits, laughing frequently and looking deep into the eyes of a friend of a friend of a friend with a yellow dress and soft lipstick. She is telling him about why she likes L.A. more than San Francisco. Interes*ted* is interes*ting*. Pay attention to her words. She is saying them, after all! They exchange numbers and we head over to the Legends Lounge. If you played in the NFL—at all, ever—you are invited. We get to the top of the elevator and come to a check-in desk, which Jake breezes past. I have to register. Wangs laughs at each formality, a high-pitched cackle that disarms the security guard.

"You played in the NFL?" they ask.

"Yes!"

They hand me an iPad and I fill out the form while trying to crack jokes through the syrup of my sloshing brain. I finish it somehow and hand it to them. They press a few buttons.

"Yep! Says here you *did* play . . . welcome!"

They hand me a lanyard and we walk into the lounge area, empty but for a few groups of guys I don't know, scattered around the top-floor restaurant. Ballers, all of them: that much is clear. That's the look that never dies.

The look may not die but the body does. My legs are as dead as a thumbtack. My muscles are failing me. I need food! Food, I tell you! They have bread with dip. They have chips. They have carrots. They have beer. That'll do.

There is a 360-degree view of San Francisco from way up here. I've never seen the city like this. It's beautiful. The sun is going down. The colors are changing by the second, reflecting off the bridges and the water, buildings and grass, sky and metal, magnifying windows and birds in flight.

The three of us pose for a photo: me between two of my old quarterbacks, Jake and Wangs, with my city in the background. Sometimes life is good. One of you assholes—throw me the fucking ball!

The sun disappears completely, words get spoken, bottles get broken, new bottles get opened. The Legends Lounge spits us out into the lobby of the Hilton. There is a bin of commemorative footballs next to a beer kiosk. Wangs grabs one on our way out and tosses it up to himself, squeezing it in his hands, lining up his fingers on the laces as we clear the double doors and hit the concrete again.

Up Market Street we walk, through the smoldering ashes of Super Bowl City, two warriors for a cause. We turn onto Eddy, then come to a stop at the crosswalk at Golden Gate Avenue. It's a hot corner, even in the middle of the night. Do you hear it? Do you smell it? Not just the junkies, not just the dregs—but the entire food chain. Dealers, pimps, prostitutes, pushers, addicts, cops, crooked cops, undercover cops, Wangs and me.

Two cars whiz by. Then another. To our right is a small corner parking lot with eight Batman-style floodlights, raised on a platform and cutting zigzag patterns across the NFL SB50 logo slapped twenty stories high on a ghetto skyscraper five blocks away.

It's game day.

Can you feel it?

"Wangs," I say, and he knows what I mean. I take off running into the empty street and look back over my left shoulder. The ball is in flight and I am the immortal man.

ACKNOWLEDGMENTS

Like all good ideas, *Fantasy Man* was conceived with smoke in the air. There was a small brush fire nearby—a beauty shop was burning. Barry Harbaugh and I stood and watched the flames curl into the sky.

"I just got back from a fantasy football draft," I told him.

"You play fantasy football?"

"Yeah."

"You should write a book about fantasy football," he said.

"Ya think?"

"Yeah."

Barry's idea, not mine. I went home and squirted out seven thousand words and sent them to Alice Martell, my agent, who passed them to the editor of this book, David Hirshey, at

Harper. David twirled his mustache and came back with a piece of paper for me to sign. All right then, go write a book!

You have six months.

So I wrote it. And it pulled me all the way in, all the way down, just like it's supposed to. Writing unleashes the enemy within. You must then kill it, or broker peace, depending on the day. All days bloody.

> One word and then the next,
> Footprints in the wilderness—
> Tracks that I can't cover;
> When they come for me,
> I'm dead

Eventually the NFL season was over and all the scenes were written. Time to edit! Time to hand over the baby. Editing happens in New York. Hirsh and I sat down in Room 725 at the Ace Hotel and pencil-fucked (circumcised) what was then called *Killing Peyton*. Barry happened to be in town. He'd stop by, throw another brush on the fire and pull up a seat. It wasn't long before we were debating whether a joke was "sexist" or arguing over the use of "vasodilation" or pondering the inclusion of the word "downscalator." (Once we found a place for "upscalator," it was decided.)

Some of the heated discussions involved passages about publishing. I find the process of creating a book—this *thing* that you're holding—interesting, exciting, even! But Hirsh doesn't. He thinks the nuts and bolts of his job are of no interest to a reader. He doesn't want to bore them. Funny joke. He couldn't be boring if he tried.

With his arm in a sling from a recent shoulder surgery, David Hirshey kept the pace during long hours at the desk, then walked the streets in search of the perfect raw burger and a cold Stella, then smoked a penalty kick past a kid in Central Park before we continued along the path discussing the book, connecting loose threads, trimming the bonsai tree.

By now, Hirsh, you are gone from that gray place; the land of cigarettes and cell phones. You can smell the Pacific Ocean from your toilet now. I can almost see you, stepping outside in the morning sun; yep, there you are—looking up at a palm tree and twirling your mustache: California Vape-Douche.

The artwork in this book is badass. It brings the story to life. And it was created by my older brother, Tom. Tom is a conduit. Anything artistic, he conduit! Whatever he touches is given timbre, rhyme, and essence. He did these sketches in L.A. traffic on his way to and from work. Elephant shoe, brother.

It is some perversity in me that forces me to this keyboard: ceaseless but harmless to everyone but me. Until it prints, that is! Then my friends are pelted with the rotten fruits of my tortured whimsy, and that shit ain't fair. I get it. They're leaving their hearts in my hands. For that I thank them all—everyone who appeared in *Fantasy Man*, especially the guys we got to know in our Bunny Five-Ball league, of whom there is now one fewer with us.

Our brother Twomp died in the spring. He has moved along to play Five-Ball in the sky. He wasn't meant for this place anyway. We'll miss you, Anthony, but don't worry—we'll always give you the number one pick.

And we know who you want.

Oh yeah! And a big thanks to the fur-ball that made this all possible: Bunny. Keep hoppin', my brother. I'll be seeing you.

ABOUT THE AUTHOR

Nate Jackson is the author of the *New York Times* bestseller *Slow Getting Up*. He played six seasons in the NFL as a wide receiver and a tight end. His writing has appeared in *Deadspin*, *Slate*, the *Daily Beast*, *BuzzFeed*, the *Wall Street Journal*, and the *New York Times*. A native of San Jose, California, he now lives in Los Angeles.